PRAXICAL LEADERSHIP

PRAXICAL LEADERSHIP

the craft of moving others, and ourselves, toward a better future

Nelson Coulter

Praxical Leadership:
The Craft of Moving Others, and Ourselves, Toward a Better Future

Unattributed quotations are by Nelson Coulter.

Copyright © 2016 Nelson Coulter
Published by MoeNel Publishing, Girard, Texas
Printed by Createspace, An Amazon.com Company
All rights reserved.
ISBN-13: 9781537685717
ISBN-10: 1537685716

Library of Congress Cataloging-in-Publication Data
Coulter, Nelson.
Praxical leadership: The craft of moving others, and ourselves, toward a better future/ by Nelson Coulter.
Includes bibliographical references.

Table of Contents

The Author

Nelson Coulter has been a learner and teacher in the field of leadership for almost four decades. Professionally he has served as teacher, coach, mentor, principal, school superintendent, and university professor. His service includes work in public schools that were quite diverse: large and small, rich and poor, predominantly Anglo and predominantly minority, all levels of campuses PK-12. Coulter teaches for both Wayland Baptist University and the University of Texas at Austin, as adjunct professor. Coulter now serves as professional consultant, author, professor, and rancher. He currently lives with his wife, Janie, in the rolling plains of West Texas, very near to his children and grandchildren.

Cover

The photo on the cover of this book is but one sample of the photographic prowess of Betty Monson. Not only is Betty a great friend and valued professional colleague, she is a remarkable artist.

Other Titles By Coulter

Leadership Tools for School Principals: Organizational Strategies for Survival and Success (2010)

Acknowledgements

I know of no one on this planet who has been more blessed than me. No, I'm not wealthy (in terms of dollars). No, I've never served in high political office. No, I haven't inherited vast holdings. What I have received, though, is unfailing support from family and friends through a lifetime of learning and growth. Moe (my lovely bride of 39 years now) has consistently counseled me, shaped me, followed me, forgiven me, and loved me, as we have edited our lives together. There is no person on the planet whose opinion and thinking I value more.

My parents and my two daughters have also been extremely influential, the first as non-judgmental and consistent advocates and the latter as loving co-learners who have forgivingly grown *with* their dad for over three decades now. And, the girls have now added two draftees (i.e., husbands) and five additional mentees (i.e., grandchildren) to our learning posse.

Finally, I want to acknowledge the women who have powerfully shaped me. I have already mentioned Moe, my lovely bride. I have also referenced above my two daughters, Summer and McKenzie, who have become remarkably capable mothers and professionals. My mom, Dian Coulter, has been with me from the start – literally, figuratively, intellectually, emotionally, spiritually. She is one of the smartest people I know, and I count it primary among my many blessings to still have her "in my court." Gladys Vest Coulter Wright Pearson, my paternal grandmother was and continues to be, though deceased, a guiding influence. Not a day goes by that I don't "feel" her presence and gentle spiritual nudge, keeping me grounded in the things that are most important. Finally, Joanne Deaver, who worked with me in two different professional settings. Joanne has been an unabashed and relentless supporter, defender, critic, and cheerleader for me, even when she probably shouldn't have. One could ask for no greater friend. Additionally, she has graciously lent her thinking to this book by way of editing help and commentary.

All of these women have shaped me, improved me, and made me who/what I am. To all I owe a debt which I can never fully repay. I love you all.

Disclaimer

I have learned greatly from the writing, speaking, and thinking of many others. And, I have exercised in this text due diligence in attributing the ideas, thoughts, and words of others accordingly. Per the Copyright Disclaimer Under Section 107 of the Copyright Act of 1976, allowance is made for "fair use" for purposes such as criticism, comment, news reporting, teaching, scholarship, and research. Fair use is a use permitted by copyright statute that might otherwise be infringing. Thus, use for non-profit, educational or personal purposes, such as works of this nature, are clearly protected under the "fair use" provisions.

As well, I have purposely endeavored to share with you what I have learned thus far in my life, as it relates to leadership. I make a number of assertions that I currently believe to be true and accurate. Please understand that I am an educator by trade and by training. I am not, and do not proclaim to be, a physician, a psychologist, a nutritionist, a kinesiologist, nor any other type of credentialed professional. I have simply chosen to share with you what I've learned and what I currently believe, for the sole purpose of sharing my learning with you. It is my great desire that you gain something useful and meaningful for your own learning and growth, both professionally and personally.

Finally, the sources I reference throughout this book are writers, thinkers, and professionals whom I deem to be trustworthy and well intentioned. Some clearly operate outside the mainstream of thought. I am quite comfortable with that dynamic; in fact, I often find myself drawn to that kind of thinking and thinkers. However, I would never cite, recommend, or invoke the thinking of those whom I believe to be shysters or fringe lunatics.

Introduction

"Act always as if the future of the Universe depended on what you did, while laughing at yourself for thinking that whatever you do makes any difference."

BUDDHIST PROVERB

Leadership is a topic that has been written about extensively. Leadership conferences abound. Leadership style surveys proliferate. Books about leadership could fill the Grand Canyon. Why does the practice of leadership demand so much of our collective human psyche?

I have been studying leadership, both formally and informally, since I was a seventh grader. At that point in my life I first became aware of being drawn into leadership roles. With each subsequent "appointment" I became more intent on learning as much as possible about leadership in order to be more effective in those roles. As decades passed I came to understand leadership more as a manifestation of service to others rather than some privilege or honor.

The thoughts and ideas you will encounter in this book are a mash-up of some of my personal dot connecting and sense making, the reprinting of some of my blog posts (you can find those at www.nelsonwcoulter.com), and a synthesis of the writing and speaking of many wise thinkers.

Leaders are the busiest, most overscheduled, and time-starved people on the planet. The constraints on their reading time are onerous. Thus, I have chosen a format for this book that is akin to a stream-of-consciousness type of flow. Consequently, the content is delivered in short sections, with lots of bulleted thoughts. Providing substance, in a succinct way, was my goal throughout. This formatting style also lends itself readily to team book studies, where the short yet concept-dense sections provide fallow ground for rich discourse and debate. Despite the lack of a continuous flowing narrative, I trust you'll find the more crisply packaged thoughts, observations, and stories to be quite congruent with the chapter titles.

The reference section at the end of this book provides a listing of the books, articles, and videos that have had significant influence on my thinking and behavior. To be sure, there are hundreds more that I didn't list, but the works you will find cited are those of thought leaders who have stretched my thinking, and thus, have shaped my behavior.

This book is, more than anything else, about how we possess the ability to chart our own lives. Like the writer of a novel, we must have a general idea of how we want the story to end, even if we don't yet know all the details and sub-plots along the way. Donald Miller (2009) speaks eloquently of this in his book, *A Million Miles in a Thousand Years*, in which he details the power we have to "edit our own lives.

Framing The Leadership Journey

"I start with the premise that the function of leadership is to produce more leaders, not more followers."

- RALPH NADER

Praxical

About the word "Praxical." You won't find it in the dictionary. I made that word up, and here's why. The word "praxis" has been in the literature for some time. It refers to the practical application of theory in ways that help us achieve our personal or organizational goals. Most of us have experienced the lack of congruence between espoused leadership theories and deployed practices. Though I greatly value theory, this book will not drag you through endless theories on leadership. Rather, I have written this book for practicing (or aspiring) leaders. I am a practitioner leader, not an academician. The word "praxical" is meant to imply the sweet-spot intersection between theory and practice. It's where the application of relevant theory actually results in effective practice. In effect, praxical suggests the blending of theoretical science with applied science.

Praxical Leadership is my attempt to demystify the intersection between practice and theory. Theories are what we derive to explain phenomena, to make sense of things. They are our attempt to identify the conditions of causality.

Once we have conceived of some theory, then we can go about the business of trying to prove that that theory applies in practice. Some theories pass muster against those tests, some don't. The theories that hold up under repeated tests of scrutiny are the ones that ultimately become useful guides for our behavior and thinking.

Many folks have advanced degrees in leadership studies of one sort or another. Those learned individuals generally have substantive knowledge in the areas of leadership theory. I have discovered through the years that countless other fine folks have earned unofficial degrees in leadership practice, the school of hard knocks, if you will. Their wisdom is no less valuable to us practicing or aspiring leaders than is that of those who have the diplomas on their walls. I strive herein to acknowledge and leverage both, since both provide critical knowledge and skills essential to effective practice.

Golf

Praxis, that intersection of theory and practice, is where the most effective leaders I know operate. They strive for that sweet spot of knowledge and skills, in order to be the very best leaders they can be. Consider golf as an analogy. I played golf for over four decades. Through that time I would sometimes play with folks who might show up in flip-flops, cut-off jeans, and baseball caps turned backward on their heads. Many of these golfers would use mismatched clubs they had purchased in garage sales or flea markets. They could stand over a golf ball, take a swing at it, and hit it beautifully, time after time. When asked how they could perform so skillfully, they would look at me blankly and say something like, "I don't know, I just hit the ball." These golfers are examples of having remarkable skills, but being devoid of the technical knowledge or an understanding of the theories behind the performance.

Then there were the golfers on the other end of the spectrum. This group would have the most expensive and trendy clubs on the market (often trading clubs yearly), they would be dressed to the nines, they would use only high-dollar golf balls, and they would have at their disposal a myriad of technology (or paid caddies) to help them assess things such as windage, lay of the land, direction of turf growth, distance to the pin, etc., etc. In short, they would have studied and leveraged all possible knowledge and theories related to high performance golf. Many of these golfers, however, could not sweetly and consistently stroke a golf ball, no matter how hard they tried. In short, they were long on theory and short on skills. They had the knowledge of golf, but lacked the ability to effectively put it into practice.

The very best golfers I knew were the ones that effectively merged theory and practice, knowledge and skills. They studied and understood the game, *and* they exhibited remarkable prowess at putting that knowledge into play effectively. It is that very intersection of theory and practice that we will seek, in this book, in order to better understand the construct of leadership.

Nature vs Nurture

A great deal of leadership debate and literature has been centered on the issue of Nature versus Nurture. Are leaders born or are they developed? The answer, I believe, is "yes." It's both. Leadership is both a disposition and a developed skills set. Both can be changed, but ONLY by those who are self-aware, who are intellectually astute, and who are committed to disciplined growth. Is that you? That shift in disposition or skills is not something someone else does to you; it is yours to cause, or not. And, the work is never complete.

Leadership, in my view, amounts to influencing others in such a way that they act or perform in ways that they might not of their own accord, or to do so at a different pace than they would otherwise. The assumption I make is that each of us wants to live a life that is meaningful, with a sense of being effective in our navigation of its sometimes treacherous currents. This is especially true of leaders, because, by the very essence of leadership, the lives of others (sometimes *many* others) are impacted by our own.

Any book about leadership is in some ways a pipe dream. The people who decide to read such a book generally do so out of some aspiration for self- or organizational improvement. Substantive ideas along those lines move the reader-leader from the realm of pipe dream toward the consideration of real possibilities.

Leaders must be seen, first and foremost, as humans. They must be able to connect on a personal level with stakeholders in all quarters. This is as much as anything an exercise of skill in the interpersonal realm.

Is effective leadership as simple as knowing who you are and what you believe? No, not quite that simple. Leadership is NOT about what we do to others; it is always about our own thinking, our own behaviors, our own beliefs. Others will follow if we are sufficiently attentive to those elements.

Profiles in Leadership

What do we want from our leaders? When asked, folks respond with a menu of laudable qualities. Words like responsible, respectful, contemplative, industrious, persevering, optimistic, courageous, compassionate, adaptable, honest, trustworthy, and loyal begin to enter the conversation. Really, it's the same kinds of thinking, behavior, and attributes we want for our own children. Who wouldn't want to possess those qualities?

The tricky part, of course, is embedding within ourselves the habits that bring life to those qualities. Leadership is partly about what we do, partly about how we do it. Mostly, however, it has to do with our inner condition, how well we are anchored to our values, how deeply we know what we believe, how attentive to and focused on the big picture we are.

Effectiveness

Effectiveness is our personal assessment of how well we are doing. As leaders, our effectiveness has rippling implications for tens, hundreds, potentially millions of others. Our effectiveness as leaders is directly proportional to our ability to stay balanced in both our public and private lives. This book is largely about how to achieve and maintain that balance.

But, what are the dimensions of leadership that need to be balanced? John Gardner (1990) divides the attributes of leadership into these categories:

1) Physical vitality and stamina,
2) Intelligence and judgment-in-action,
3) Willingness (eagerness) to accept responsibilities,
4) Task competence,
5) Understanding of followers/constituents and their needs,
6) Skill in dealing with people,
7) Need to achieve,
8) Capacity to motivate,
9) Courage, resolution, steadiness,
10) Capacity to win and hold trust,
11) Capacity to manage, decide, set priorities,
12) Confidence,
13) Ascendance, dominance, assertiveness, and
14) Adaptability, flexibility of approach.

While that is a rather daunting list, he adeptly captures the comprehensive nature of the construct of leadership.

Our effectiveness as leaders is the level of alignment between our intentions and our subsequent impact. The late Stephen Covey (2004) provided an excellent road map for us in achieving that public-private life balance:

1) Be proactive,
2) Begin with the end in mind,
3) Put first things first,
4) Think win/win,
5) Seek first to understand, then to be understood,

6) Synergize,
7) Sharpen the saw, and
8) Find our voice and inspire others to find theirs.

Every musical work in the history of man has been composed from the same menu of musical notes. Yet, the new, the remarkable, the good, the bad, and the "different" continues to be composed in every corner of the planet, every day. Leveraging those same old notes in new ways, in new combinations, in new arrangements continues to generate extraordinary compositions, seemingly without end.

As well, the same menu of human emotional "notes" have been at our disposal through the millennia – love, anger, trust, fear, happiness, sadness, joy, hope, and surprise. While they, too, are just the same old notes, we have great latitude in creating a new experience for both ourselves and others.

As previously mentioned, Donald Miller (2009) posits that we have the power to "edit our own lives." Indeed, we do. We get to assemble, rearrange, deconstruct, control the rhythms, and the volume of our emotions every minute of every day.

How are we composing those notes in new and remarkable ways? After all, it *IS* our lives we are composing. And, as leaders, that composing has direct impact on the lives of others.

Full Range of Leadership

One of the most influential books I've encountered on the topic of leadership is *Improving Organizational Effectiveness Through Transformational Leadership* (edited by B.M. Bass and B. J. Avolio, 1994). Bass was a prolific empirical researcher of the construct of leadership. A quick Google or Wikipedia search will provide you a plethora of works he has authored.

In my view his most powerful contribution to the study of leadership is his **Full Range of Leadership Model**, which is a conceptual "lens" through which we can view the construct of leadership. Below is a quick summary, with the highest effectiveness models at the top of the list, sequentially diminishing as you work your way down:

- **Transformational Leadership** - the leader impacts followers through four operational leadership skills - 1) idealized influence, 2) inspirational motivation, 3) intellectual stimulation, and 4) individualized consideration.
- **Transactional Contingent Reward** - followers compliantly do what the leader wants, and get rewarded for doing so.
- **Transactional Management-by-Exception (Active)** - the leader actively monitors for deviances from expectations in follower behavior/performance, then reacts punitively when violations are identified.
- **Transactional Management-by-Exception (Passive)** - the leader does not actively monitor for deviances from expectations in follower behavior/performance, but when those come to his/her attention, punitive responses follow.
- **Laissez-faire** - the complete avoidance or absence of leadership.

We can probably all think of concrete examples of leaders we've known that align with each level. The more important response is to examine carefully our own behaviors, thinking, and skills, and work actively to move our daily performance toward that **Transformational** level.

Who Are the Leaders?

In the literature there are hundreds of definitions of leadership. Here's mine: *Leadership* is the act of influencing the thinking and/or behavior of others.

That process can be used for good or evil purposes. It is practiced in both intentional and accidental ways. It is exercised both formally and informally. Leadership is manifested through a wide array of acts/words (modeling being the most powerful medium).

Here are a few of the places/roles where we see leadership at work:

Playground	Parenting	Clubs
Teams		Organizations
Churches	Friendships	Schools
Grade Levels		Workplaces
Teachers	Coaches	Siblings
Families	In the mirror	

Leadership is at play wherever and whenever two or more humans interact with each other. (As a rancher, I see the same dynamics at place in the animal kingdom, but that discussion belongs in a different book.) And, in virtually every circumstance of life, you and I are either playing the role of *leader* or *follower*.

As we consider the concept, and those social arrangements I noted above, please ask yourself these two questions:

Who are the leaders I follow? (and why?)
Who are the folks who follow my lead? (and why?)

Each day, we make some important and defining choices on both sides of that ledger.

Cotton Candy

Over the years I've observed organizations that have had all kinds of folks in leadership roles. I suspect you have, too. Some of those leaders remind me of cotton candy.

Their persona is attractive and sweet, yet vacuous and inconsequential. Their words are lofty and their ideas are often noble. Yet, they repeatedly fail to manifest grit, dependability, steadfastness, and trustworthiness. On the contrary, they often prove to be hollow, sometimes bogus. Time and again their actions fail to align with their words.

In effect, they represent a pretty and delicious temptation, hanging on nothing but thin air. Just like cotton candy.

For those of us who choose to be leaders of substance, we must build into our lives and thinking the habits that will "brand" consequential principles onto the fleshly tables of our hearts. We must become *students* of leadership, and engage in a deliberate pursuit of being better, every day.

Resume Versus Eulogy

David Brooks (2014) makes some powerful points about *why* we live and *what* we choose to live for. Some of his assertions include:

- When life becomes a "game" to us, we lose ourselves.
- Resume virtues are the skills we bring to the marketplace.
- Eulogy virtues define who we are in our depth (love, consistency, boldness, etc.) and the quality of our relationships.
- Depth of character is constructed through fighting/wrestling with our "signature sin," from which all the others emerge.
- We can only "save" ourselves by hope, by faith, by love, and by forgiveness.
- Resume virtues are focused on the short-term, self-centered rewards while eulogy virtues are focused on timeless, others-centric behaviors/ thinking.

As we look inward and take honest assessment of ourselves, we will assuredly see that there's still quite a lot of work to do in order to become our best selves. When we purposefully engage in that work, the eulogy virtues persistently begin to trump the resume virtues.

Cluttered

One of the challenges of living in this age of pervasive technology is that we can accomplish SO MUCH MORE! We can read more, watch more, have more Facebook friends, send/receive more email and instant messages, conduct more phone calls (on multiple phone lines), attend virtual as well as on-site conferences, and interface instantly with our work colleagues around the clock through multiple media portals. Add to that the endless "homework assignments" we receive (because we are so efficient), the vacation days that somehow go unused, the family events that get attended virtually through Skype or texted videos, the working breakfasts/lunches/dinners, etc. The list goes on and on.

Why is it that so many efficiency tools seem to make for less and less efficiency? The clutter seems overwhelming. And, in fact, it is. All this clutter conspires to make us less effective and less self-actualized in some of the most important things in our lives.

So, what's a 21st century leader to do? Achieving and maintaining balance has and always will be a challenge for leaders. That is nothing new. Achieving balance is especially difficult for those of us who fit into that "driven" category. As the old saying goes: "If you focus on everything, then you focus on nothing."

To unclutter requires the discipline and courage to step back and stand down in order to make some significant choices. Here's a nice recipe:

Decide this: How will you measure your life? Determine a few (not a lot) of things that you value deeply and that move you intellectually/spiritually/physically. Think of these as the things the folks who eventually stand around your grave will be thinking in relation to your accomplishments. (Don't think of these as metrics, but rather as standards).

Once you have that SHORT list determined, write it down. Codify it somehow; have it tattooed backward on your chest, write it on the bathroom mirror, use it as a screen saver, or employ some other convention to get that menu of must-dos in front of your eyes daily. Yes, they are important, but they will get swallowed up by clutter if you don't keep them constantly in front of your eyes, heart, ears, and mind.

Let go, lovingly and kindly, of the tasks, requests, homework assignments, etc., that do little to move you in the direction of those standards. In some cases this will mean saying "no" to some jobs/tasks/assignments/requests that come your way and in some cases it will mean simply choosing to make a "C" instead of an "A" on some of those assignments.

Share this list of "the things that matter most to me" with others in some way. It will help both you and those that know you understand and accept the ways that you are no longer willing to spend your time.

This process is difficult. But, we can do it, and we *should* do it. Our lives will be measured by it.

Leadership's Work

Leadership guru Steve Farber (you can find him here: http://www.steve-farber.com/), quotes Terry Pearce of the Haas Graduate School of Business (University of California, Berkeley) regarding the challenges of bold leadership: "There are many people who think they want to be matadors, only to find themselves in the ring with two thousand pounds of bull bearing down on them, and then discover that what they really wanted was to wear tight pants and hear the crowd roar."

Sample (2002) makes a similar point in his book titled *The Contrarian's Guide to Leadership,* in which he articulates the difference between *wanting* to be a leader and actually being willing to do the messy work that is associated with it.

To be sure, when we make the choice to follow a path of excellence, both for ourselves and our organizations, the challenges are many and daunting. It is not work for the faint of heart. But, oh the fun and adventure of the journey...

Leadership Hell

All leaders have frailties.

Leaders who know their own limitations and are willing to openly admit them are the ones with the most authenticity. By virtue of knowing ourselves, and "owning" our weaknesses, we come to understand that leadership is not a singular construct. Leadership is a collective endeavor, simply because leadership requires followership.

The best organizations (regardless of size or scope) are the ones in which the leaders and followers understand themselves *and* each other well. They're the ones in which all members know that their individual contributions *really* count when it comes to accomplishing their goals. The leaders of those organizations freely invite those with complementary strengths and skills to provide the work/thinking/contributions that the leader can't. Those leaders are also the ones who typically serve up recognition and praise in large doses.

Leaders who try to hide their own shortcomings and shift blame dishonor and disrespect the contributions of others. They tend to complain and commiserate about the others in the organization "not carrying their weight," when, in fact, the leader has created the conditions that cause others to stand down, to withhold, to coast, to hide.

Those kinds of leaders live in a hell of their own making............and should.

Uninformed

Several years ago, I was chairing a leadership team meeting one day in the organization of which I was the chief officer. As was often the case, I was engaging this group of highly trusted and very competent leaders in dialogue about how best to meet the needs of our customers.

During the course of that leadership team dialogue, one of the team members took exception to a proposal that I offered for consideration. That was not at all an unusual situation. Still isn't, for that matter. I was not offended by the pushback. In fact, I believe it to be a quite healthy organizational environment in which debate, give-and-take, rebuttal, and dissent are protected and safe practices.

In this instance, the objecting colleague accused me of being "uninformed." Not "misinformed" nor "misled" nor "mistaken" nor "misguided." Nope. "Uninformed." Ouch! That hurt.

No, I didn't bristle or curse or nip the colleague back. I genuinely *want* feedback and pushback and healthy debate. I firmly believe that the best and most-likely-to-succeed decisions come from rigorous discourse. In this instance, I had clearly hit a nerve with my colleague.

The assertion that I was "uninformed" did, however, cause me pause for deep reflection. If I was truly uninformed, or even perceived to be uninformed, then I had work to do, on a personal level. I either needed to learn more (in order to *not* be uninformed) or I needed to articulate my position more effectively (in order to not be perceived as uninformed).

That experience was a good double-barreled lesson for me. I needed to do two things:

LEARN MORE and COMMUNICATE BETTER.

Believing and Caring

When we look back through history at powerful leaders who have had a huge and lasting impact on others, we can see a couple of common indicators:

First, those consequential leaders believed uncompromisingly in their cause. Though they may not have understood completely where their leadership would ultimately "take" the tribe (in fact, few leaders know this), they believed strongly in the tenets, the vision, the rightness of their *direction*.

Second, those powerful leaders cared deeply about those who followed them. The best of our leaders understand that many sacrifices are made along followership's path. Those sacrifices translate into one thing - *commitment*. None of us have enough time/energy/effort/resources to do everything that is important. Choosing to invest in a particular vision or cause implies choosing *not* to spend our time/energy/efforts/resources on some other ones (even though they may be very worthy ones). The best leaders understand the commitment behind those choices and reciprocate with *care*.

Authentic leaders understand that forced compliance is not leadership. When others volunteer to follow a cause/vision, their best efforts follow (even without compliance elements like excessive monitoring, sanctions, penalties, score cards, hierarchies, etc.). When folks are coerced or forced into followership, their best efforts rarely ensue.

As leaders, two important questions follow:

1) How deeply do I believe in the rightness of the direction/vision I'm pursuing (and trying to get others to follow)?
2) How much do I care (and show it) for those who choose to follow along?

Who Built That?
Learning is a layered, intertwined, interdependent process. It occurs in fits and starts, and refuses to follow a steady trend line. There are virtually NO new ideas or thoughts. Every "new" idea/concept/finding/product is built in one way or another on previous work and knowledge.

This concept is known as constructivism. Our knowledge and skills do not spring solely from some content to which we were exposed (perhaps via a teacher, a mentor, a video, a friend, some software, etc.). What really makes learning "stick" is the *context* within which we learn it and within which we use it. Most of us can peel a banana; few of us can tell how, or from whom, we learned that skill. We each "got there" through different pathways.

Such is all learning. Constructivism cuts to one of the coolest things about learning – it's personal and customized (and too often not intentionally so). There are interesting implications here for those of us who would like to teach something important to our children, our grandchildren, our students, our colleagues, our followers. Context matters, A LOT! In particular, those of us who lead others are, fundamentally, teachers of those who follow us. Understanding how learning occurs and how it can be more effectively caused is a critical component to our success as leaders.

Relationships

The attention of leaders must always be on relationships, and the fruitful management of those relationships:

> relationships with/between organizational members,
> relationships with/between organizational divisions,
> relationships with/between competitors,
> relationships with/between suppliers,
> relationships with/between the complex and mediating variables that exert pressure on the organization from without and within.

RELATIONSHIPS are everything when it comes to being effective as leaders.

As with a study of the water cycle, it is impossible to say which has the most powerful influence on the environment - the rain, the runoff, the water table, the evaporated moisture, or humidity. So is it impossible to clearly define which has the most impact on the other, the leader or the followers. Both shape the other, both are shaped by the other, all while within the milieu and contexts of their world. What is important is that both leader and organizational members be continually learning. They should be aware of that mutual shaping process and engage it with intentionality.

True synergy and power are nested in the interwoven and networked relationships and in the cultural frequencies through which the members of organizations and communities communicate.

Changing Me

Change should not be discomforting to us. We can learn to accept change as the norm. Change continually happens around us, in the form of technological advances, political winds, social arrangements, fashion trends, and the like.

Sometimes, however, we will feel the need to change ourselves. That need usually springs from one of the following:

- A desire to be or get better, somehow.
- The realization that we've been wrong in some way, and need to rectify it.
- The need to adapt to evolving external factors.

Emotion and social trends may trigger the need for change in ourselves, but they are not sufficient to sustain such efforts. The need must be something deeper and more substantive.

Two questions drive our decision for intrinsic change:

1) Is there concrete and irrefutable evidence that we need to change?
2) Will we be better servants to others as a result of the change?

Well-intentioned change makes us better (which is a good thing).

Women's Ways

From my 45-year study of leadership, one of the most comprehensive compendiums I've read on the topic is *The Handbook of Leadership* by Bernard Bass (1990). (If you're a leadership junkie, you may want to add this to your library.) I referenced Bass's Full Range of Leadership Model earlier in this chapter.

From my study of Bass and numerous other authors who have written about transformational leadership, I became convinced that I had some serious gaps in my own leadership skills. I concluded that my effectiveness as a leader could be improved if I could grow myself in areas of leadership that Dr. Bass declared to be more naturally acquired and practiced by *women*. Yep, Bass said that women leaders prove to be more dispositionally inclined to operate within those transformational leadership constructs than do men.

Thus, I set out to learn more about women's ways of leading. I know it sounds strange to hear that from a southern country boy, but that journey has proven to be most gratifying for me. Trying to learn and practice women's ways of leading has made me a much stronger leader in the following ways:

- I am much more inclined to operate from a collaborative worldview.
- I listen more and talk less.
- I better understand the emotional connection between leaders and followers.
- I very rarely issue mandates, directives, or ultimatums.

To be sure, I'm nowhere near where I want to be as a leader. There is much yet to be learned and mastered in the practice of that occult art. But, I'm thankful to Dr. Bass and many others who were bold enough and giving enough to point me in the direction of improvement.

Success Accelerant
Trust is the accelerant that boosts the likelihood of success.

Trust in our team.
Trust in our leaders.
Trust that our product performs.
Trust that our suppliers will deliver.
Trust that improvement is part of the deal.
Trust that our services will be deployed with integrity.

Trust that tomorrow brings more and better opportunity.

Trust that all have carried out their assignments with fidelity.

Trust that all involved will honor commitments (written/spoken/implied).

Disruptions in trust have the same effect as trying to run uphill. It can still be done, we can still "get there," but not without a lot of extra effort and energy.

What is trust built on? *Relationships!* Relationships founded in integrity, dependability, fairness, commitment, and transparency. There is a direct connection between our prospects for success and the relationships we build and nurture.

Process of Learning

The year was 1988 and I was a math teacher, athletic director, and head football coach at a school on the rolling plains of Texas. The assistant superintendent of that school asked me and three other faculty members to attend a workshop in April of that year. The training was intended to help schools meet the needs of at-risk students.

I agreed to attend. Only then was I informed that the training would be a whole week in length. Yep, five whole days away from my math students and athletic teams during the month of April. That's a tall order for an educator. I began to have second thoughts about participating, but stuck with the commitment anyway.

I learned a lot of important stuff that week, but one thing stands out clearly as pivotal in my pursuit of betterness. Each of the five days of that training the presenter began the day with exactly the same sentence: "This is a process, not an event."

He understood that the folks in that training were each working in different organizations, with different contexts, with different students, and working from different experiences personally. In effect, he understood and overtly stated daily, so that we would begin to understand, that learning is a process. It has no beginning point, and it certainly has no ending point. It occurs in fits and starts, and it is inseparably intertwined with our personal contexts.

I learned a great deal that week. The most profound lesson for me was the realization that LEARNING (mine and yours) is a *process*, not an event.

Leave the Script

We try and try to make organizations run according to "script." In fact, they don't - never have, and never will. Life, passions, tragedies, markets get in the way and often run averse to the script. Our view of organizations would be better served if we thought of them in terms of improvisation (like improvisational comedy). Critical to success is our ability to adapt, to take the prompt and run with it, to avoid balking, hesitating, and resisting, and rather, to say "yes, and…" more often than "but,…"

Scripts are well defined, and rigid (completely ignoring the context and feedback loops). Improvisation, on the other hand, is driven by strong underlying principles of contextual awareness, adaptation, cooperation, and flexibility.

It is principle-centered leaders, not the script-driven, that will sustain and prosper over time.

Miracle Grow(th)

Early in my professional life I served as a high school football coach. One of my players (let's call him Tom) came into my office one morning during our August two-a-day workout sessions. Tom informed me that he was likely to grow 5-6 inches and gain 10-20 pounds by week's end. *Now* he had my full attention; I immediately began asking questions.

Tom had gone home after the previous day's workouts, completely exhausted. His mother had mixed several gallons of green liquid and left them on the kitchen table. Tom assumed his mother had prepared Gatorade to replenish his electrolytes after an exhausting day of football practice. He quickly downed one gallon and was working on a second one when his mom entered the room and began yelling at him. Her concoction was not Gatorade after all; rather, it was Miracle Grow, which she had prepared to feed her flowers and plants.

Optimistically, Tom concluded that if Miracle Grow could work such wonders on plant life, then he could expect commensurate biological dividends from his consumption of the same.

No, Tom didn't add five inches in height nor 15 pounds of body weight in the next week or month or year. That growth only occurred *after* he graduated, of course.

My point? Grow we should (personally and professionally), but it is never the result of magic potions or shortcuts. Affectatious growth is the result of a deliberate "fitness regimen" which we prescribe for ourselves and engage in with daily discipline. Of course, we have the option of NOT "growing" ourselves in those dimensions (and many folks make that choice).

What is not available to us is a magic elixir (such as Tom's mistaken belief that drinking Miracle Grow might provide some sort of physiological shortcut to Amazon-ness). The old saying of "inch by inch, life's a cinch" applies to our personal growth. We get to prescribe the menu, the regimen, the routine, and the growth most assuredly follows. Or NOT, if that's what we choose.

This book is about reflective leadership practice. Experience doesn't mean much of anything if we don't learn from it.

As we get started on this learning journey together, please take a moment to jot down three questions that are at the forefront on your mind regarding leadership and your practice thereof:

1)_____?

2)_____?

3)_____?

2

Servanthood: The Noblest Endeavor

"The greatest among you will be your servant."

- JESUS CHRIST (MATTHEW 23:11,
NEW INTERNATIONAL VERSION)

Moral Imperative

The moral imperative that underlies leadership is service. Any aspiration for leadership or exercise thereof that is not grounded in desire for service is egocentric, if not narcissistic. When leaders lose sight of the objective of service, we drift inevitably into the disastrous territory of selfish motivations and self-serving decisions. We have seen this play out historically time and again with dictators and kleptocratic states. The first step in the downfall of an organization is when its leaders begin to cannibalize the constituents.

While service is not always a choice, such as in the cases of slavery and conscription, for leaders it is a choice – the fundamental choice. Aspiration and ambition are the constant companions of leaders. To overcome those constraining forces we must resolve to dedicate our talents to noble purposes, always in the interest of serving others.

The essence of life is finding and living for meaning. Service, more than any other human endeavor, provides us with that meaning. Others-focused leadership must always trump self-serving interests (Block, 1993).

Even beyond being a servant, as leaders we must take the long view and teach a service mindset to others as well. If we fail in the transmission of the service centered orientation then we have doomed the generations that follow to selfish consumption and a shallow existence. As Oren Lyons, Chief of the Onondaga Nation is credited with saying, "We are looking ahead, as is one of the first mandates given us as chiefs, to make sure and to make every decision that we make relate to the welfare and well-being of the seventh generation to come. . . ."

As servant leaders, we must continually keep that seventh generation in our sights, even as we make the decisions that impact our followers and our organizations today, in this moment.

Cover Bands

In the book *Die Empty*, Todd Henry (2013) makes the interesting point that "cover bands don't change the world."

I've heard many cover bands over the years. Many were not just good, they were EXCELLENT. Some seemed capable of playing famous songs even better than the original artists could. Most of those cover bands were populated by superb and skillful musicians and vocalists. Most had extraordinary stage presence. Many of them had skills that verged on unbelievable.

There is nothing wrong with legally copying, mimicking, cloning the exceptional work of others. In fact, there are very few new ideas, new combinations of notes, new arrangements of words, new efficiency processes, etc. We are wise to "copy" what works.

We are unwise, however, to bury our own creativity and innovation by investing ourselves *only* in replication. Few of us will literally "change the world." Yet, we all hold the prospect of changing *our* world. That best happens when we spend some of our precious time/energy/effort chasing something we are passionate about. That's when we try something different, make ourselves learn something new, take a risk, or, in the words of an old song, "dance like nobody's watching."

Few of the iconic artists/artisans set out to change the world. Their work was/is almost always about the artists' attempts to fully express themselves. Muhammad Ali is famously quoted: "Service to others is the rent you pay for your room here on earth."

Living a life of service is perhaps our best chance to "change the world." We become our best selves when we dedicate our efforts to helping others achieve their best selves. It's called living fully.

Postal Service

In a global economy, those who provide goods and services must do so in a way that is responsive to the marketplace. Consumers want good products/services at a fair price, and they want variety and choice in their options. They want those products/services right now! And, they want those products/services to have a degree of customization and personalization.

When entities of any kind focus on their internal processes rather than on the customer's desired outcomes, they essentially choose to make themselves irrelevant to current and potential clients (i.e., market share).

Across organizational genres, the global economy opened up marketplaces – it has provided variety, choice, customization, personalization, relevance, and affordability to those who previously did not have the option of "shopping."

Just as the U.S. Postal Service has evolved itself into a black fiscal hole (noble intentions, perhaps, notwithstanding), many self-serving entities seem to be working themselves toward the same end. (I am not picking on the Postal Service out of some particular malice. There are numerous governmental entities I could use to draw the same analogy).

To quote former Speaker of the U.S. House of Representatives, Tip O'Neill, "All politics are local." His point was that local issues and local politicians were the real drivers behind regional, state, and national issues, not the other way around. I would argue that the same is true across the organizational spectrum, though we seem to have been engaged in a decades-long experiment of trying it the "other way around."

The U.S. Postal Service has found itself in an untenable position fundamentally because it failed to adapt to the changing needs and desires of its client base, preferring to continue with the model that was created for a different era. The U.S. Postal Service got into this predicament precisely because it viewed itself as the only option for its client base. Any leader and/or organization that continues to act as if we have a captive audience and perform as if we need not be responsive to the needs of our current clientele (not the clientele that existed 10, 20, or 30 years ago) *SHOULD* expect customers to leave. (Recall the fall of Blockbuster and the demise of Polaroid, to cite just two examples of death by adaptive paralysis).

Wise leaders craft organizational cultures centered on service – adeptly serving the needs of its customers. It's a messy and challenging process, but those who achieve such cultures will be greatly rewarded, in all respects.

Service as Gift

Service to others is the most powerful gift we can give. Service is rendered in many forms:

- Teaching others what we have learned.
- Helping others accomplish worthy goals.
- Sharing our God-given talent often and in many ways.
- Helping others develop to their fullness.
- Trusting others.
- Connecting others to enlarge their network.
- Affording others opportunities to grow.
- Ministering to others who have suffered or are in need.
- Listening, without judgment.
- Forgiving, as needed.
- Loving, unconditionally.

Once we are the beneficiaries of such service, we are then compelled to both reciprocate and radiate the same, within our circle of influence. The size of that circle of influence is immaterial. The enactment of that service is immensely consequential.

To serve in that manner is to approach life in its fullness. To withhold service is the fountainhead of decay.

Improved Serve

In many organizations, a typical knee-jerk reaction to poor service to customers (whether they be buyers, students, vendors, or volunteers) is to try to put a new policy/regulation/rule in place to "fix the problem!"

The "problem" is almost always a failure in the human interaction component, often manifested as dysfunctional or nonexistent people skills. Trying to automate our way out of interacting with customers diminishes both customers and employees. Our customers deserve better, and our employees can do better (if taught/coached/trained/allowed to do so).

Why not invest a little time in developing the troops with regard to improving people skills? And, why not incentivize (I'm not talking money here, but rather, with recognition, praise, affirmation) exceptional instances of service?

Both sides of this human interaction equation benefit from quality service delivery, and no one loses. Really. Talk about win-win solutions! What is the biggest barrier to taking this approach to service? We have to be willing to listen to and get to know our customers.

The time to get started on it is NOW!

Big Box-itis

I've been doing some reflecting of late on my buying habits. I've developed real concerns about my inclination toward bargain hunting. To be sure, I can save money by buying in volume from the folks who ship and stock the desired products in mega-bulks. I've noticed that, despite the fact that I can usually get the products for a *really* cheap price, problems inevitably emerge if/when I need some kind of assistance in relation to the product(s).

The Big Box Boys don't seem nearly as interested in (or even capable of) helping me when the table saw they sold me has a malfunctioning on-off switch. They cheerfully put me on hold, bounce me from department to department (if not country to country), and ultimately tell me that I can re-box and ship the whole darned thing back and they'll replace it.

The problem is: I wanted/needed the saw this week (or today). I don't need a whole new saw. I just need a little troubleshooting help.

Because of scenarios like that, I am more frequently buying from the "little guy," who knows a lot about the products he sells. It gives me comfort to feel confident that the seller can actually tell me things like where the on-off switch connects to the power, how the pump works when it's down in the water well, where and under what conditions those vegetables were grown, how one kind of tire will perform versus another, etc.

The Mom & Pop folks are increasingly getting more of my money (if I haven't already driven them out of business, that is). And, I'm okay with it. The service they provide seems every bit as important to me as the product itself.

In that same line of thinking, we should consider how to hone our own skills at providing service in our chosen areas of vocation. I'm pretty sure that's what will keep the "customers" coming back (or not).

The Off Brand of Toilet Paper

One of my favorite bloggers, Seth Godin (you can find him here: http://sethgodin.typepad.com/), frequently reminds us that cheaper is rarely better, easiest is rarely bestest (my word, not his). We see proof of those assertions often when we reactively reach for the cheapest priced product (soap, tires, computer, insurance, barbed wire, software, lawn mower, etc.), only to be hugely disappointed by the quality or the durability of our chosen item, or the fidelity of the vendor when we need remedy.

To be sure, the age of interconnectivity, automation, easy access to information, and convenient transportability allows businesses and institutions to remove a lot of the traditional costs of overhead and middlemen, in order to get their product or service in our hands at the lowest possible price. These changing paradigms are having a huge impact in all areas of business.

At the end of the day (and the transaction), what brings us satisfaction and happiness is almost always the fact that the product/service did what we needed it to do, when we needed it done, with the least amount of inconvenience or discomfort. To channel Godin again, the wisest businesses, institutions, and individual vendors (we *ALL* fit into at least one of those categories) figure out ways to optimize the exchange by optimizing the experience.

Two elements are the "trump cards" with regard to customer satisfaction: **Relationship** and **Quality**. Think of these two elements as the vehicles of service.

Most of us are just fine paying a tad bit more, if the transaction is immersed in those two elements. It seems rather odd that we so often abandon those two powerful dimensions for the sake of saving a few cents or a few dollars.

Relationship and **Quality.** If you've ever wrestled with a discount insurance company, you understand the importance of the first. If you've ever used the off brand of toilet paper, you understand the second.

Customers

We *all* have customers.

Customers are those who want or need something we can provide. Those provisions take the form of goods or services or expertise or support. Our customers may pay for those provisions with money, or with currency of some other kind (such as bartered goods or services or expertise or support).

We *all* have customers.

They may be complete strangers whom we encounter in a business exchange. They may be close acquaintances who need/want something we can deliver. They may be family members. They may even be our bosses (yep!).

We *all* have customers.

No matter what our age, our occupation, our interests, or our avocations, we are in the daily business of providing *something* to others that they need/want from us.

We *all* have customers.

If we deal with our customers from a mindset of service, they will dependably reciprocate and return their "business" to us gladly in the future. If we deal with our customers from a mindset of obligation and entitlement on our part (assuming they have no other options), we'll lose their business. We'll also lose the many blessings that would otherwise be ours.

How we treat our customers is an excellent predictor of what we can expect out of life. The choice is ours (as usual.)

Bleacher Cleaning

In my first high school principalship, I invested a lot of time and effort in "coaching" our student leaders on the campus. I steadily hammered them with the concept that "to whom much is given, much is required."

As part of that leadership coaching process, I encouraged our cheerleaders to make sure that they removed and appropriately disposed of the spirit signs they would hang on the bleachers and fences at the stadiums of our opponents. After a couple of games, I noticed that our band pitched in and began cleaning up their portion of the bleachers, too.

It wasn't long before I started receiving letters from principals, superintendents, even political officials from the communities we competed against, praising our students for their acts of service. Of course, I shared those letters with our students and faculty. Shortly thereafter, I noticed that our cheerleaders and band, of their own accord, began "sweeping" the whole side of the stadium we occupied when we played elsewhere. They combed the bleachers from end to end, cleaning them of all trash and debris. Surprisingly, even many of our community members began joining our students in those acts of public service.

Watching that dynamic of infectious leadership centered on service to others, triggered by the student leaders in our school, is one of the highlights of my years of service as an educator. The memory of watching those students sweeping the bleachers after a game (win or lose) still makes me emotional. They were enacting one of the purest and simplest forms of servant leadership.

But then, aren't *ALL* acts of authentic leadership rooted in the soil of service?

Empowerer

The most impressive leaders I know understand and employ the element of empowerment. They do so by acknowledging the varied gifts that others bring to the endeavor. They work diligently to craft work assignments that allow those others to "display" their gifts daily. They persistently articulate the vision, the goals, the mission, and the successes to those ends - in many and authentic ways.

Those leaders are *empowerers*.

Beyond that, they celebrate the growth and progress and success of others. In fact, they revel in it. They go out of their way to help others be successful. They craft meaningful growth opportunities for others. They say "thank you" in a million ways (with no strings attached). They always give more than they take. The centerpiece of their thinking is service to others.

That's what *empowerers* look/feel/smell like.

We could use a few more leaders of that ilk. No credentials are required. You can start anytime you're ready.

MEANING(less)

Philosophers, thinkers, poets, and sages have for centuries attempted to define the meaning of life. Most notably, Holocaust surviving psychiatrist Victor Frankl chronicled his experiences in German concentration camps in *Man's Search for Meaning* (1946). It is a powerful and compelling work in which Frankl offers his insights on that topic. Thousands of other books, stories, and legends detail the lives of men and women who searched for life's meaning in their own way.

No, I don't have the ONE answer to what gives life meaning. However, I'm pretty sure that we only realize meaning in our lives when we get beyond our-selves (spiritually speaking). As a habitual observer of life and those who live it (both gracefully and not so), I think I can identify a very powerful attractor (to steal from the lexicon of physics) for providing meaning to life.

It seems to me that those who engage zealously in service to others enjoy lives that are full of meaning. Conversely, those who are most committed to

themselves, their own fortunes, their own comforts, and their own needs are the best representatives of living lives that are meaning*less*.

Leader Types

Leaders come in a bazillion varieties: bosses, generals, moms, presidents, Sunday School teachers, CEOs, coaches, managers, officers, parents, preachers, siblings, etc. You know them, you interact with them, you watch them, and in most cases you *ARE* them, in one form or another.

Of the best leader types I know, some of the common manifestations/behaviors I see (and admire) in them is that they:

- Are slow to anger.
- Listen before they speak.
- Keep their eye on the BIG picture.
- Treat *EVERYONE* with respect.
- Have spines made of steel (they honor their commitments/responsibilities relentlessly).
- Have strong wills but soft hearts.
- Constantly seek to serve others, somehow, some way.
- Are fundamentally modest and self-deprecating.
- Seek solutions that benefit all (rather than win-lose solutions).
- Are voracious learners.
- Give more than they take.
- Exhibit vulnerability and practice total transparency.

What a list! Plenty to aim for, huh?

Insulation

In construction and in clothing, insulation protects us from unpleasant, even painful, stimuli. Those stimuli come in the form of cold, heat, wind, rain, intense sunlight, etc. Moderate amounts of all that stuff is actually rather pleasant, but when experienced in extremes a little protection is most appreciated.

Many leaders attempt to "insulate" themselves from interaction with customers, both internal and external. They go to great lengths to make themselves unavailable to the folks within the organization and to customers of the organization. Sometimes they insulate themselves by putting in place layer upon layer of organizational hierarchy, each level serving as a filter to mitigate bad news or unpleasant feedback before it climbs to the next layer. Sometimes, leaders actually create physical barriers between themselves and their stakeholders. These insulators show up in the form of inaccessible offices (often on the top floor), gatekeepers whose role is to intercept and redirect "intruders" (and visitors), huge desks behind which they hide/sit (usually in high-backed and elevated chairs). All these techniques serve to insulate the leader from unpleasant elements.

But why?

If things are going poorly (or well, for that matter), shouldn't the leader want a firsthand account of it? If processes/systems are malfunctioning (or performing beautifully), shouldn't the leader want to know about it early on? If there is a disgruntled customer (or a raving fan), shouldn't the leader need to hear directly from them?

The best leaders I know walk the halls, they talk directly to customers, they drink coffee with the custodian, they visit the loading dock, they sit in the waiting room, they ride with the delivery guy, they answer the phone, they *ENGAGE* with the stakeholders, at all levels.

These leaders are most cognizant of the fact that service translates as accessibility. These leaders also understand that organizational insulation will keep them well "protected"...........and in the dark, right up until the time the ship begins to sink.

Stages

> "All the world's a stage,
> And all the men and women merely players;
> They have their exits and their entrances,
> And one man in his time plays many parts,
> His acts being seven ages."

This quotation by Jaques in *As You Like It* (Act 2, scene 7, 139-143) is one of William Shakespeare's most oft-quoted passages. Without going into a deep literary deconstruction, the passage clearly alludes to the fact that we are mere actors on the stage as we live our lives. We play many parts during our life-time, and we play them out on many stages.

Here are the stages some of us "play" on:

- Working on a factory line.
- Caretaking a special needs child.
- Teaching a class of students.
- Managing a small business.
- Participating in family life.
- Presiding over the most powerful nation in the world.

Few of us control the stage upon which we play. Few of us could have pre-dicted the "stage" upon which we play. All of us can choose to play upon that stage with aplomb and skill. All of us can perform our role in a way that makes the world a better place (regardless of whether we're playing to an audi-ence of one, or 6,000,000,000).

Serving others well, regardless of the stage(s) we play on, is a very worthy undertaking. And, like acting, our *craft* can be polished, revised, improved every day. Preferably with intention and attention.

Mrs. Smith's Angels

I came upon a one-car accident about 20 years ago. On a very hot July afternoon, an elderly woman had lost control of her car on a remote west Texas highway (about 30 miles from the nearest community). The vehicle had rolled several times, coming to rest in the ditch. I was the fourth person to come upon the accident. Three other men had arrived on the scene ahead of me, two of them brothers who were traveling together.

As I approached the scene, I found the other men attending to the elderly woman. She was out of her vehicle, seated on the ground. She was badly shaken, with abrasions around her face and head, and bruising already evident on her arms. I assumed there were other possible injuries that were not visible.

The woman was clearly rattled and kept asking for her glasses. Three of us began searching the path that the rolling car had traveled through the weeds and grass, trying to find her spectacles. One man stayed with the woman to console her as we waited for an ambulance to arrive. After several minutes of combing through the weeds, we found her glasses.

As the woman put her glasses on her bloodstained face, we were all huddled around. As she regained her visual bearings her eyes went wide. She could now clearly see our faces. She gasped, and choked down a sob, then exclaimed, "Kenny! Bobby!" Then and only then did the two brothers, both in their forties, look closely at her face. They, in unison, cried out, "Mrs. Smith!"

Mrs. Smith had been the Sunday School teacher for Kenny and Bobby when they were children, some 30 years earlier, in a town that was about 100 miles from the scene of the accident. Kenny and Bobby had had no contact with Mrs. Smith since they had graduated from high school and moved on in life.

Tears began to flow (among all five of us) as the awareness of the situation began to sink in: Mrs. Smith's investment in the spiritual development of two young brothers some 30 years earlier had come full circle in the two "angels" being on the scene at her time of direst need.

Reminds me of the song by Alabama, "Angels Among Us."

Reminds me, too, of all the angels that have littered my life-path. Some have been most obvious. All have service as their primary mission. Most, I am sure, unbeknownst to me. Sure hope I've done right by them all…

Trudy's Line

Nobody likes long lines. And, few of us will choose to stand in a longer line if a shorter one is available. Thus, Trudy's story…

While I was principal of a large high school many years ago I observed a most puzzling behavior on the part of our students. Many of them were *choosing* to stand in longer lines to pay for their lunch. Since the school was so large, we had a mall-type food court with a bank of six checkout registers. Each day I noticed that the checkout line at Trudy's register was always longer than the lines at the other five registers. This made absolutely no sense as all the registers were the same, and students could pay out at any of the registers.

As time went by, and as I got to know Trudy personally, I came to understand. Trudy was very near retirement age, yet her personality and spirit were absolutely vivacious. She laughed and smiled freely. She seemed to know each student by name (in a high school of 2800 students). Not only that, but Trudy would fully engage with each student she was ringing up – commenting on their hair, complimenting their shoes, asking about their day, etc.

Trudy, purely and simply, made each student feel like they were the center of the universe.

It's not that the other cashiers were mean or unpleasant. Trudy simply served as an emotional magnet for students in that school that could feel very large and impersonal. What a remarkable testimony to the power of interpersonal connectivity and service-orientation.

Funny thing is, I found myself standing in Trudy's line more often than not, too.

She also knew *my* name.

She made *me* feel better, too.

Thanks to Trudy for teaching me some *VERY* important lessons about serving others.

The Space Between the Notes

I once had a conversation with a highly successful musical director (I'll call him TA). We were discussing our love of music. In particular, we were talking about how some performances "move" us, and some just seem to be nice and well-played renditions.

TA commented that the element that sets magnificent performances apart is not the fact that the musicians play the notes well (since that is what musicians are supposed to do). TA asserted that the truly distinguishing element in those moving performances is not the notes themselves, but the "space between the notes" with which the performers impose their influence on the composition. In effect, a script (in this case, the musical score) becomes a work of art in the hands/minds/renditions of masterful artisans.

Seems to me that the same holds true in our work lives. We can simply go to work each day and follow the script, play the notes, teach the students, interact with the customers, go through the paces. For such we receive pay-checks, nods, bonuses, and occasional affirmations.

OR, we can choose to take those scripts and embellish them with powerful adaptations like smiles, pleasantness, helpfulness, customer-focus, authentic presence, empathy, service-orientation, and the gift of our attention, turning our work into a daily work of art.

It's the spaces between the notes (i.e., our embellishments of service orientation) that really make the difference for both the performer (us) and the listener (our customers, our colleagues, our students).

"Never Take More Than You Give"

One of my favorite songs is "Circle of Life" (by Tim Rice and Elton John). It's on the "Lion King" sound track. (You can view and listen to it here: http://www.youtube.com/watch?v=o8ZnCT14nRc)

My favorite line in the song is this: "You should never take more than you give."

Life is fullest when we commit to serving others, in ways both small and large. That concept is nicely captured by the lyrics of Rice and John. The world is a better place when we give more than we take.

Leadership is about service to others, purely and simply and most righteously. It is the act of giving. Many who charade as leaders with motives more aligned to achieving notoriety, gaining wealth, acquiring fame, and wielding power are what I consider to be counterfeit leaders. Selfishness and egotism are the drivers underneath their actions.

Leaders of integrity, however, "give more than they take" every day, in the interest of two goals:

1) Make the lives of others better, and
2) Make the world a better place.

Indeed, service is about giving more than we take. Blanchard and Hodges (2005) speak of the two roles of servant leadership: 1) Visionary Role – in which we help collectively set the course for our organization, constantly communicating to our followership collectively who we are and where we're going; and 2) Implementation Role – in which we constantly keep ourselves and our followership focused on serving, always in the interest of noble endeavors, noble intentions, and noble acts.

As always, we get to choose (how we will live, how we will lead, who we will follow). What better choice than service?

3

Fitness for Service

"Who we are at work is our life. Who we are in life is our work."

- PETER BLOCK

Reflections

Like it or not, leaders (their thoughts, dispositions, and proclivities) are reflected in the organizations they lead. Moxley (2000) describes it as the leader's "shadow."

The cover of this book depicts a beautiful reflection off of the water. Similarly, the persona, the belief systems, and the character of leaders reflect onto the organization. Consequently, it is critical that we, as leaders, come to understand ourselves. Even more importantly, it is incumbent upon us to think very carefully about "who" we want to become.

Our personal fitness has direct bearing on the organizations we lead. The very health and wellbeing of those who follow our lead is impacted immeasurably by our own health and wellbeing. With that interdependence of health in mind, we now begin to explore how to achieve optimal health.

Our Triadic Selves

Think of personal holistic health as a triad of three fundamental dimensions: emotional/spiritual, intellectual, and physical. All taxonomies and categorizations are human inventions conjured to help us better understand complexities. Thus, please know that discussing ourselves in those triadic categories is a convention that, by its very nature, oversimplifies the complex interplay among and across those dimensions. None of those triadic components can be thought of as being independent from the others. What we eat affects how we think. How we exercise impacts our emotional state. What we learn intellectually informs our choices regarding relationships and physical health. The extent of this interconnectedness and interdependency is unquantifiable.

Our emotional/spiritual selves are the source of our groundedness, the basis from which flows our character. In essence, it is this dimension of our lives that gives them meaning, and a sense of contribution (both now and into the future). The intellectual dimension is, in effect, our mind. Note, however, that the mind is not the same thing as the brain. The mind is the repository of our cumulative knowledge, the museum of our memories, the curator of our learning, and the center of our consciousness. While our intellect represents the rational side of our existence, it is in no way limited to facts, figures, and data. Our intellectual health is implicitly connected to our emotional/ spiritual health and to our physical health. Finally, the physical dimension is our structural self. While we often think of our physical health in terms of muscles, skeleton, and external appearances, we are increasingly coming to new understandings about the impact of nutrition, environmental contexts, and emotional/spiritual health on our physical wellbeing. We are whole people, and consequently, must attend to our fitness from a holistic perspective (Covey, 2004).

This chapter is intended as a provocation. I attempt, herein, to challenge your thinking and assumptions about health and wellbeing, knowing full well how much that health and wellbeing impacts the people in the organizations you lead. That said, we must attend carefully to our own health and continual development in all three dimensions. That caretaking must be thoughtfully considered, deliberately prescribed, and diligently deployed. We must sanctify the necessary time to "grow" ourselves in all three dimensions. Scheduling time to attend to each of the components is critical, as it reinforces the absolute necessity of fitness in each dimension.

When we make ourselves as healthy as possible, the organizations we lead stand the best chance of achieving optimal health.

Who Are You? Who Do You Want to Be?

As we consider our triadic selves, the first step is to take a careful assessment of who we are now. Reflection is the ground in which wisdom grows. The reflective process involves stilling the mind, stilling the spirit, stilling the body. Reflecting on what we believe, why we believe it, and the habits that drive our daily behaviors can provide critical insight into who we are right now.

Once we have taken that snapshot of who we are, then some critical questions follow:

> Am I who I want to be?
> If not, what needs to change in my life to move me toward who I want to be?
> If so, what next steps in my development will take me to ever higher levels of health and effectiveness?

As Donald Miller (2009) aptly asserts, we get to write and edit our own life stories, for the most part. Fundamentally, our fitness is about being disciplined in the development of each of the triadic dimensions of our lives. Through the implementation of very purposeful habits, we can begin molding ourselves into who we want to be.

Learners First

The fundamental key to our growth is *learning*. Regardless of whether we're talking about the emotional/spiritual, the intellectual, or the physical dimensions, learning is the precursor to growth. The three keys that trigger that growth are reflection, exploration, and engagement. We can achieve higher levels of "intelligence" within all three dimensions once we commit ourselves to a path of growth. Howard Gardner (1993) interestingly defines intelligence as the ability to solve problems that one encounters in real life, the ability to generate new problems to solve, and the ability to make something or offer a service that is valued within one's culture.

Never before has it been easier to learn. The Internet alone has placed within our reach the sum of all human knowledge. Powerful search engines and databases have greased the skids of research to the point that all we need do is type a simple question into a search box and a myriad of resources are instantly dropped onto our device screens. As Rodney Smith notes (in Brady, 2003), "When we are committed to learning for its own sake rather than accumulating knowledge, every experience becomes a teacher." (p. 261) As a result, our learning is not limited to breadth *or* depth, it can be accelerated through breadth *and* depth.

We err in using the excuse of being too busy to attend to our personal growth. That diversion is akin to claiming we're too busy to eat or to sleep. As leaders, we simply cannot function effectively without attending to our holistic fitness. Leaders are pressed for time more than most. Recall the old adage that "fatigue makes cowards of us all." This applies to the triadic dimensions of our health, and subsequent performance, too. Fitness prepares us to be successful. It does not make us successful in and of itself. Success is as much about perseverance and resilience as it is anything. Fatigue is the antithesis of perseverance and resilience.

Health, Wellbeing, and Leadership

The health and wellbeing of the organization is a fundamental responsibility of leadership.

The "nutrition,"
the "exercise,"
the emotional fitness,

the condition of the social contexts,
the quality of the working and learning environment,
are all "health markers" that must be monitored and attended to by
those in positions of leadership (whether we're talking about a family
of three or an organization with 1,000 employees).

Not only is it important to monitor the data on those markers constantly,
it is also necessary to make decisions proactively in the interest of achieving
optimal "health" on each of those indices. "Health" is far easier to manage
proactively than "illness" is reactively.

If we, as organizational leaders, are not attending effectively to our own health
and wellbeing, there is little chance we can effectively attend to the health and
wellbeing of the group.

Metabolism

A fundamental process in the human body is that of metabolism. It is the
confluence of chemical/biological reactions and interactions occurring in our
bodies that cause us to move, to grow, to digest food, to expend energy, to absorb nutrients, to reproduce, to heal. Evidence of metabolism can be observed
at the cellular level, in our individual organs, and in our integrated physiological systems.

In effect, metabolism is a process of taking inputs and converting them to outputs. We take in, then metabolize, air, food, water, minerals, etc. The quality
of the performance of our bodies is directly attributable to the quality of the
inputs that get metabolized.

We also metabolize experience (Cloud, 2010). Our minds and our spirits
absorb experiences of all kinds and metabolize them. As with the physical
stuff, the resulting quality of intellectual and emotional/spiritual performance
is directly connected to the quality of the inputs.

So, what we read, who we associate with, what we listen to, how we move, the way we worship ALL MATTER. Good stuff in, good stuff out.

Chew on that for awhile. (Pun intended.)

Doing-Being

What we do defines us. Our habits make us who we are. Not the other way around. Habitually getting angry at people/circumstances/customers/bosses defines us as an angry person. Habitually expressing gratitude defines us as a grateful person. Habitually serving others (from acts as small as opening a door for someone to those as consequential as spending our vacation teaching sustainable gardening to those in poverty) defines us as servants.

The good news is that we can change who we are by changing what we do (i.e., our habits).

Two questions are telling:

1) How do others define us? (Or, stated another way - What do others expect from us based on their observations of us?)
2) Who do we want to be? (Or, stated another way - What habits must we abandon or adopt in order to become who we want to be?)

We don't have to get permission to begin personal revision, and we can begin whenever we're ready.

Out of Gas

I've only allowed myself to run out of gas in a vehicle on a couple of occasions (fortunately). When it has happened I've been extremely irritated at myself because I let it happen in the first place. It's not like monitoring the fuel gauge takes significant effort. The gas gauge is right there before our eyes. It is easy to see the gauge moving toward "empty."

The most inconveniencing thing about running out of gas is the amount of time/effort/expense associated with getting refueled. Phone calls have to be made, friends or family inconvenienced, roadside service procured, gas cans carried down the road, judgmental looks from passersby absorbed, etc. All because we were *too busy* to refuel when we were running low.

The same thing can happen to us spiritually, emotionally, intellectually, and physically. We can tell, usually through a variety of "fuel gauges," when we are depleted. It's not like it sneaks up on us. And, it's not like we can keep going when we have depleted ourselves (just like the car can't keep going when it runs out of gas).

And, just as with a vehicle, there is huge time/effort/expense associated with the corrective actions required when we let ourselves "run dry." Lost productivity, damaged relationships, poor performance, loss of bearing, compromised health, brain fog, even hospitalization, can be the effects of letting ourselves "run out of gas."

So, what is your "gas gauge" telling you right now?

Imperfection

Learning occurs best when we understand that there are many right answers to most real-life kinds of problems. Learning environments that allow for mistakes to be made safely, for corrections to be an assumption, where complexity is the norm, where imperfect (but improved) prototyping is the standard menu, are the best ones for optimization of learning.

No essay (or blog post) is perfect.
No experiment is flawlessly replicable.
No project stands as the sole exemplar.
No performance is without room for polishing.

Somehow, conditions and contexts always impose themselves on the environment and the outcomes, making solutions to real-world problems elusive and chock full of variation. Only in using tightly restrictive, simply answered, carefully controlled "testing" systems can we declare one's work "perfect." These results are most often declared on standardized assessments, with limited answer options, and easily agreed upon "correct" answers. Oversimplified but easily graded assessments/evaluations are illusions of authentic learning, not manifestations of authentic learning.

Such is *not* the way of life, living, work, or art. Imperfect, but improving *IS*.

Excellence

Excellence (or the pursuit thereof) almost always entails some angst. It may come in the form of commitment to change, confrontation, making controversial decisions, restructuring, remaking, retooling, learning something new, unlearning something now obsolete... On the other hand, non-excellence is rather easy to achieve. Mediocrity and averageness are achieved mostly through continued breathing.

When we make the conscious decision to live life in a more excellent way, it implies then a process of constant self-assessment (either for us as individuals, or the organizations in which we hold membership). Attempting to view ourselves, our current performance, our level of effectiveness in a fair and objective way essentially raises a mirror to our shortcomings, flaws, and failures, as well as our "wins," attributes, and successes.

What we have learned from research on human behavior is that making some kind of public commitment triggers an inner determination to work toward an espoused goal, to become that person, to fulfill that resolution. Psychologically, we become "married" to our commitment and begin reshaping ourselves (even unconsciously) into the image we have publicly proclaimed to pursue.

The choice to pursue excellence is also rather liberating. It's like giving one's self (or the organization) permission to break from previously held assumptions or constraints (in all their dastardly forms) in order to create something better, newer, different, magical.

Golden is the fact that we don't have to ask anyone's permission to pursue excellent living. We can unilaterally decide to learn more, act more humanely, attend to our fitness more deliberately, love more deeply, and serve others more richly.

Why would we not?

Competence

Most of us want to feel competent – competent in our work, competent in our relationships, competent in our hobbies and passionate pursuits. But, how do we gain competence? How do we get to that place where we know what we're doing, understand the process to accomplish those endeavors, and are respected in our management of those pursuits?

Competence springs from a web of entangled variables:

- *Learning* we achieve through reading, listening, and engaging with knowledgeable others.
- *Practice*, practice, practice at using the talents and attributes with which we have been blessed.
- *Skills* developed purposefully through disciplined growth.
- *Wisdom* gained through reflection on experiences (the experiences are rather worthless unless we *learn* something from them).
- *Insight* acquired through stretching our own limits, with the associated successes and failures (no pain, no gain, no competence).

Competence is NOT derived from titles or money or privilege. It cannot be bought. It cannot be faked. Competence cannot be conferred on one. It has to be earned, and no one else can earn it for us. Finally, competence is not an end in itself. No matter how "good" we get at doing stuff, knowing stuff, applying processes, the competence only has real value when we're using it in service to others. Otherwise, we are only competent narcissists.

Manufacturing

Our best selves are manifested when we employ all three life dimensions (emotional/spiritual, intellectual, and physical) into our endeavors. It is from such integrated and holistic enrollment that we experience wholeness and self-actualization. However, it is often the case that we bring only two of those dimensions to our workplace: the intellectual (our mind) and the physical (our body). When we do that we rob ourselves and our vocation of the very driver of creativity, innovation, and service, which is the emotional/spiritual dimension.

When we invest only our mind (i.e., knowledge) and our body (i.e., physical structure) into our work, we allow ourselves to become little more than automatons or machines. In essence, we simply function as robots, in the business of "manufacturing."

EMOTIONAL/SPIRITUAL FITNESS

Our emotional selves and our spiritual selves are inextricably intertwined. Our emotional/spiritual wellbeing is really about fitness of the "heart." Put another way, that emotional/spiritual duality is our "soul," the embodiment of our consciousness, through which our principles and morals are manifested.

Psychologists generally agree that there are a number of basic human emotions. What they don't agree on is how many there are. We are told there is somewhere between four and over 60 human emotions (depending on the researcher or author). Prominent among those emotions are love, joy, surprise, anger, sadness, and fear.

Deepak Chopra (2009) advises us that the health of our souls is manifested in several ways:

1) When the link between us and the God of our understanding feels liberating, rather than constraining,
2) When we are able to love, given and expressed freely, it is as if it awakens our soul,
3) When we understand that our soul is boundless (unless we constrain or restrict it, which we often do),
4) When we accept that grace is the freeing byproduct of our surrender to full awareness, and
5) When we accept that we are fully the Universe and the Universe is fully us.

Just as with our physical health, there are health markers by which we can monitor our emotional/spiritual fitness. Chopra (2009) provides an outline of just such a menu of health markers:

"You will know that you are responding from the soul level whenever you do the following:

Accept the experience that's in front of you.
Approve of other people and yourself.
Cooperate with the solution at hand.
Detach yourself from negative influences.
Remain calm in the face of stress.
Forgive those who offend or wrong you.
Approach the situation selflessly, with fairness to all.
Exert a peaceful influence.
Take a nonjudgmental attitude, making no one else feel wrong." (p. 182)

Self-Regulation

The ability to self-regulate is the hallmark of individuals and organizations that are healthy, vibrant, have longevity, and are self-sustainable. Our moods are the external manifestation of what is going on in our emotional/spiritual dimension. Being able to regulate our emotional/spiritual selves, and thus the moods we exhibit (which are contagions, according to Bono and Ilies, 2006), is fundamental to optimizing our wellbeing.

Daniel Goleman (1994) speaks to the importance of what he describes as emotional intelligence. According to Goleman, our emotional balance is derived from the ability to self-regulate (once we're sufficiently self-aware) and to gracefully manage relationships with others (once we've become adept at being aware of and empathetic toward them).

Relevant to the discussion of emotional/spiritual fitness is the idea that the responsibility for our wellbeing belongs with *us*. It is not the responsibility of others to attend to our fitness in this regard. (The same holds true in the intellectual and physical dimensions of our lives.)

Happiness

A conversation about emotional/spiritual wellbeing must include consideration of the concept of happiness. To clarify, happiness is not the same thing as pleasure. Our happiness can be generally framed in two distinct categories, the first being Hedonic wellbeing. This is the kind of happiness that comes from pleasurable experiences, like sex, winning ball games, parachuting, etc. It's the product of experiences that give us those brief emotional highs and physical rushes. The second state is that of Eudaimonic wellbeing. This state is the result of partaking in acts of service, belonging to a cause bigger than oneself, engaging in meaningful life pursuits, spiritual grounding, etc. These kinds of activities result in feelings of peace, self-actualization, and a sense of purpose.

Martin Seligman (2002), psychologist and researcher of happiness, concludes that our happiness, and thus, our emotional/spiritual wellbeing, is best realized when we are functioning in high congruence to the six fundamental virtues held sacred by virtually every civilization on this planet. Those virtues are:

Wisdom/Knowledge, Courage, Love/Humanity, Justice, Temperance, and Spirituality/Transcendence. Seligman and his team describe what they call "signature strengths" that lie within each of those virtues. Here is how those strengths align with the respective virtues:

> **Wisdom/Knowledge:** 1) Curiosity/Interest in the world, 2) Love of learning, 3) Judgment/Critical thinking/Open-mindedness, 4) Ingenuity/Originality/Practical intelligence/Street smarts, 5) Social intelligence/Personal intelligence/Emotional intelligence, and 6) Perspective.
> **Courage:** 7) Valor and bravery, 8) Perseverance/Industry/Diligence, and 9) Integrity/Genuineness/Honesty.
> **Humanity and Love:** 10) Kindness and generosity, and 11) Loving and allowing oneself to be loved.
> **Justice:** 12) Citizenship/Duty/Teamwork/Loyalty, 13) Fairness and equity, and 14) Leadership,
> **Temperance:** 15) Self-control, 16) Prudence/Discretion/Caution, and 17) Humility and modesty.
> **Spirituality/Transcendence:** 18) Appreciation of beauty and excellence, 19) Gratitude, 20) Hope/Optimism/Future-mindedness, 21) Spirituality/Sense of Purpose/Faith/Religiousness, 22) Forgiveness and mercy, 23) Playfulness and humor, and 24) Zest/Passion/Enthusiasm.

We achieve ultimate happiness when we are fluidly operating within our signature strengths on a consistent basis. It is not hard at all to see the connections here with the idea of praxical leadership.

Worth noting also is that our happiness is a choice. Each day we get to choose happiness (or not) in the context of Seligman's virtues described above. Secondly, we are responsible for our own happiness. It is not the job of any other person, group, or government to ensure our happiness.

Finally, our happiness is most assuredly impacted by stress. All kinds of stimuli can trigger stress in us: considering death (for ourselves or loved ones), feeling self-pity, regrets, family circumstances, emotions, aging, money, navigating life, marriage, culture, forgiveness, good-byes, and graduations are just a few examples. Whatever the trigger, stress drives us toward our dispositional nature. Consequently, it pays great dividends to us when we examine upsetting situations through multiple perspectives, and make conscious decisions about how we deal with that stress. Finding ways to operate within our signature strengths (noted above) in response to stress helps us navigate it in much healthier fashion.

Groundedness

Another component in achieving optimal emotional/spiritual wellness is understanding and leveraging what grounds us. This implies coming to know ourselves deeply, as a result of very purposeful seeking and reflection. The principles we choose to live by are few and deeply ingrained. On the other hand, the skills, approaches, strategies, and tactics we choose to anchor ourselves to those principles are myriad and malleable. We tend to build our life habits with the motives of convenience and comfort, but character comes from a much deeper place. And our character, ultimately, must be the driver of our habits. Otherwise, our habits will drive our character.

Badaracco (2002) suggests that knowing who we are is the critical first step in *becoming* who we are. We can learn to overcome the restraining forces of shortsighted pride and pretension, but only with a clear understanding of their antecedents and a strong commitment to living in strict alignment with our principles. At the end of the day, our character is the evidence of our groundedness, the basis from which we make decisions. This interplay forms the nexus of our behaviors.

Leader's Responsibility

John Gardner (1990) states, "In any community, some people are more or less irretrievably bad and others more or less consistently good. But the behavior of most people is profoundly influenced by the moral climate of the moment. One of the leader's tasks is to help ensure the soundness of that moral climate." (p. 192) If we assume Dr. Gardner's assertion is correct, then the emotional/ spiritual wellbeing of leadership is critical to being able to impact the moral climate of the organization.

Effective leaders are compelled to have a high degree of emotional stability. Understanding the role and power of emotional engagement is imperative for leaders, both for ourselves and for those who follow our lead (Goleman, 1998). Emotional intelligence may be the single most important factor in the effectiveness of a leader. What is emotional intelligence? According to Goleman, emotional intelligence is comprised of four competencies: self-awareness, self-regulation, others awareness, and relationship management. Empathy also plays a powerful role in emotional fitness. Being able to put ourselves in the shoes of, or behind the eyes of, another is critical in understanding them and their perspective. Prowess in these dimensions is imperative to our ability to relate to and connect with others.

Daniel Goleman (2008) also advises us that social intelligence is key to our ability to succeed as leaders. Social Awareness refers to a spectrum that runs from instantaneously sensing another's inner state, to understanding her feelings and thoughts, to "getting" complicated social situations. That Social Awareness includes:

> *Primal empathy*: Feeling with others; sensing non-verbal emotional signals.
> *Attunement*: Listening with full receptivity; attuning to a person.
> *Empathic accuracy*: Understanding another person's thoughts, feelings, and intentions.
> *Social cognition*: Knowing how the social world works.

Social Facility refers to our ability to sense how another feels, or knowing what they intend. Social Facility builds on social awareness to allow smooth, effective interactions. The spectrum of social facility includes:

Synchrony: Interacting smoothly at the nonverbal level.
Self-presentation: Presenting ourselves effectively.
Influence: Shaping the outcome of social interactions.
Concern: Caring about others' needs and acting accordingly. (p. 84)

Russ Moxley (2000) notes that, "... our practice of leadership either suffocates or elevates spirit." (p. xii) Indeed! As leaders, our emotional and social intelligence have profound bearing on which of those two outcomes is realized.

Default Setting

What guides our thinking when things are going great? What stipulates our reactions when we're under duress or dealing with some difficulty? What guides our behavior when no one else is watching? One word is the answer to all those questions – *Character*. Our character is our default setting. When we reboot, our character is the place we start from.

So, how is character fashioned? It's the result of several things:

- The values we were raised with.
- The influence of consequential others in/on our lives.
- The choices we personally make regarding our beliefs.

What are the indicators of our character?

- Love - how we display it, how we receive it.
- Self-control - how we self-regulate mentally, physically, emotionally, spiritually.
- Integrity - how we align our actions to our beliefs and words.
- Optimism - how we see, and work toward, a better tomorrow.
- Humility - how we acknowledge and accept our own frailty.
- Courage - how we fare in the face of opposition.
- Respectfulness - how we view and treat others.
- Spiritual groundedness - how we seek and represent the God of our understanding.

Is our character set in concrete? Nope. Just like our golf swing, our reading habits, our morning routines, and our nutrition regimen, our character is, in effect, *the habitual manifestation of choices we make.*

While character is our default setting, we have the power to determine what those settings are. And, we have the power to change them if we like.

Worthiness

> Worthy work is centered in the sacred pursuit of service.
> Worthy thought stretches our mind to new levels of understanding.
> Worthy intention focuses on leaving the world a better place than found.
> Worthy worship is ever deepening communion with our God.
> Worthy learning affects greater skills and richer thought.
> Worthy speech uplifts, both others and us.
> Worthy love gives more than it takes.

Houston and Sokolow (2006) articulate eight principles they believe can and should drive the thinking, the talk, and the behavior of those in leadership positions. They assert that those principles are grounded in a spiritual understanding and can only be optimally practiced from a spiritual mindset. I would argue that there is no endeavor more worthy. Those eight principles are: 1) Intention, 2) Attention, 3) Unique Gifts and Talents, 4) Gratitude, 5) Unique Life Lessons, 6) Holistic Perspective, 7) Openness, and 8) Trust.

Improving our spiritual fitness is a daily undertaking. Our "energy" follows our attention. Our habits define our behaviors. Quite often our most powerful messages are the simplest ones. One of the common components of spiritual thought, regardless of where you find it practiced on the planet, is the theme of wholeness and interconnectedness. Leadership is about connecting dots, seeing patterns, being open to other perspectives, understanding the whole and the parts all at once, and, somehow, enabling others to do the same. As we improve our emotional/spiritual fitness we become more adept at seeing and operating from that basis of wholeness. We become better able to suppress our biases, preconceptions, prejudices, anger, and resentment, understanding that they in many ways disable us.

Pursuing emotional/spiritual fitness from the perspective of worthiness implies our commitment to betterness, growth, and building up. Unworthiness in any of those eight principles lessens us, and thus, it lessens those we influence. Always, *ALWAYS*, we get to choose.

Parasitic

Oddly, emotional/spiritual states have "life" to them. Though not organisms by definition, they seem to live and breathe and grow and evolve. They also have their own sources of nutrition, and seem to have the ability to propagate, to beget similar offspring.

Some emotions and mindsets even take on a parasitic nature. Anger is like a parasite. So is hate. So is distrust. They need a host, which they slowly but surely invade, permeate, and eventually destroy. Unless, of course, the host purges them first.

Leadership and Spirit

Russ Moxley (2000) asserts that fully engaging the spiritual/emotional component in our work creates necessary congruence. In fact, ignoring the emotional/spiritual dimension ultimately results in commitmentless work, both from ourselves and from others. Leadership exercised devoid of attention to the emotional/spiritual dimension fails to plumb the depths of organizational achievement, experiencing only the shallows as result. Fully actualizing work should bring to us a sense of life, rather than the feeling of a daily march toward death.

An environment of partnership, of community, which recognizes and invites differing gifts, skills, energies, and thinking, fosters high performance and worthy achievements, both individually and collectively. Only from honoring a diversity of viewpoints can a shared sense of purpose and meaning emerge. Only when leaders learn to create space for honest dialogue, truth finding, shared decision making, does true partnership in the leadership process emerge. Only through relationships and community do we come to fully make sense of our lives.

In many respects, attending to our emotional/spiritual fitness is about coming to deeper understanding of our beingness. When we spend more time in human *doing* than in human *being*, we begin to understand the

emptiness of the former and miss the power of the latter. Our inner life irrefutably affects our outer work.

INTELLECTUAL FITNESS

Imposter

I seem to be living the life of an imposter.

In trying to live according to the tenets of the Christian faith, I've never felt like I was quite getting it right. So, I attempted to learn more about discipleship from writings, audios, videos, and exemplary others, so that I would be "faking it" less and "getting it right" more often. Each day makes me feel a bit less the imposter, but I'm not near where I want to be yet.

In serving as a leader in various settings, I've never felt like I was quite getting it right. So, I attempted to learn more about leadership from writings, audios, videos, and exemplary others, so that I would be "faking it" less and "getting it right" more often. Each day makes me feel a bit less the imposter, but I'm not near where I want to be yet.

In being a father, son, husband, brother, grandfather, and friend, I've never felt like I was quite getting it right. So, I attempted to learn more about relationship management from writings, audios, videos, and exemplary others, so that

I would be "faking it" less and "getting it right" more often. Each day makes me feel a bit less the imposter, but I'm not near where I want to be yet.

In serving as teacher, coach, principal, superintendent, and professor, I've never felt like I was quite getting it right. So, I attempted to learn more about teaching and learning from writings, audios, videos, and exemplary others, so that I would be "faking it" less and "getting it right" more often. Each day makes me feel a bit less the imposter, but I'm not near where I want to be yet.

In being a responsible steward of the planet, I've never felt like I was quite getting it right. So, I attempted to learn more about nature and its integrated systems from writings, audios, videos, and exemplary others, so that I would be "faking it" less and "getting it right" more often. Each day makes me feel a bit less the imposter, but I'm not near where I want to be yet.

It seems the only path out of the quagmire of impostership is more *learning*. Here goes...

(Please forgive me as I continue to fake it awhile.)

Learning Journey

If we're not learning, we're dying (or already dead).

Learning can come from:

- A book/article/blog we're reading.
- Screwing something up monumentally.
- Watching an expert practice a desired craft.
- Seeking tutorials from knowledgeable others.
- Soliciting the advice and counsel of a wise mentor.
- Paying attention to the cycles and rhythms of nature.
- Asking consequential questions, of ourselves and others.
- Trying to get better at something (e.g., fishing, physics, writing, etc.).

- Reflecting on the "why," "how," and "what happened" of a previous endeavor.
- Observing someone make a mess of things (e.g., their job, their life, their children).

We often feel that we are simply too busy to "fuel our tank." I once heard the late Stephen Covey ask, "Ever been too busy driving to take time to stop and get gas for your car?" I'll bet not.

There are LOTS of ways to engage in self-directed learning. When we stop learning, we start dying.

Knowing's Forms

Epistemology is one of those high-sounding words with a much simpler meaning than any formal definition you can find for it. In layman's terms it simply means *ways of knowing*.

Many learning theorists have crafted conceptions of the way knowledge is acquired, stored, and used. Examples include Bruner (1987), Bloom, et al (1956), and Erickson (2002). I won't try to compete with those folks intellectually but I do have my own view of the way knowledge gets packaged and used by us learners.

I believe we can think of knowledge in three categories:

1) **Remembered Stuff**. This is content we remember, like the multiplication tables, our favorite dessert, and our anniversary (well, some of us remember that one).
2) **Acquired Skills**. This is procedural knowledge like how to bake a cake, or drive a car, or solve a quadratic equation.
3) *Ways* **of Thinking**. This is the abstract application of knowledge that occurs when we craft solutions to problems, when we make nuanced

choices premised on analyses, when we make valued-based judgments, or when we interpret a piece of music.

In all three areas, we can choose to sit in neutral or to push our learning, and thus, our intellectual fitness. We do that through the habits we employ on a daily basis. Additionally, we can decouple ourselves from habits that impede that learning (e.g., watching mindless television programs, unfocused Internet surfing, etc.).

Costa and Kallick (2000) propose 16 "habits of mind" for our consideration: persisting, managing impulsivity, listening with understanding and empathy, thinking flexibly, thinking about thinking (metacognition), striving for accuracy, questioning and posing problems, applying past knowledge to new situations, thinking and communicating with clarity and precision, gathering data through all senses, creating/imagining/innovating, responding with wonderment and awe, taking responsible risks, finding humor, thinking interdependently, remaining open to continuous learning. They appropriately chose the word "habits" to describe these mental disciplines, for that is exactly what they are. Any of us can adopt these habits and embed them into the daily fabric of our lives. There's nothing keeping us from beginning right now, and we'll be much fitter intellectually for it.

+/-

The human brain is a remarkable thing. The human mind is even more amazing. Philosophers, biologists, psychologists, chemists, theologians, physicists, even a few of us lay people, have for hundreds of years debated the connections between brain and mind. We struggle to make some kind of sense of where our consciousness comes from. The debate still rages.

One irrefutable fact is that the *way* we think impacts the way we behave. More than anything else, habits govern our behavior. And, we have great power to determine our habits.

One small step toward re-wiring our thinking, thus our habits, is to think and talk in positives rather than negatives. That can start with the way we think and talk about ourselves and others. There is great (and empirically-based) wisdom in the old adage, "If you can't say something nice about someone, don't say anything at all."

Some examples of positive talk (and thinking):

- I can get this right.
- She's an excellent conversationalist.
- We're a great team.

Some examples of negative talk (and thinking):

- I'm a screw up.
- He's a terrible finisher.
- They're only looking out for themselves.

Our thoughts govern our words govern our behaviors govern our words govern our thoughts govern our behaviors govern our thoughts...

All that recursive wiring and re-wiring has direct impact on outcomes, both for us and for those who follow our lead.

Cross Pollination

We sometimes get "stuck" in our work life, and even in our personal life. I believe one cause of that stuck-ness is due to becoming insulated within one worldview or kind of thinking.

In both our work and personal lives we tend to associate with the same folks all the time. We go through the same motions almost every day. We use the same software to do our work. We walk and drive the same paths repeatedly. In fact, it seems we have the same conversation(s), over and over and over.

Certainly, having some sound routines that produce good results is hard to argue with. However, what frequently happens is that we tend to approach the same problems, go through the same processes, talk with the same people, day in and day out. We lose our sharpness, we lose our freshness, we lose our enthusiasm, and we lose our curiosity.

Stepping out of our comfort zone is an excellent catalyst to "sharpening our saw," as Stephen Covey would call it. I often read books written by people who don't do work anything similar to mine. I'll watch videos of folks whose worldview is completely different from my own. I'll strike up conversations in airports or hotels with folks who look, smell, talk differently than I do, just to see what I can learn from them. Even when I go to conferences that are within my own professional genre I usually seek out and sit at a table with folks I don't already know, just to see what I can learn from them.

Meeting and engaging with these unfamiliar things/others almost always forces me to:

1) Be extra attentive,
2) Ask good questions, and
3) Listen carefully.

That's a very useful triad, *IF* my intention is to learn something I didn't know. Which it is.

Not Knowing

There's nothing wrong with not knowing, unless we're satisfied with not knowing. Not knowing is at its best when it serves as the impetus for finding out. Not knowing is at its worst when it serves as the final buzzer on our desire to know.

We have a choice each time we are confronted with not knowing. We can decide we want to know more about a topic/skill/issue/concept, or we can decide we don't care enough about the topic/skill/issue/concept to seek germane knowledge.

I have repeatedly chosen not knowing over knowing when it comes to working on automobiles. I have repeatedly chosen knowing over not knowing when it comes to trying to understand how the learning process works. We all make those important choices. Our time and energy are finite. What should be alarming to us is when we choose not knowing almost all the time.

Learning new stuff is invigorating and empowering, and it makes us better leaders.

Intellectual Leadership

As leaders, we simply must "know our stuff." Because of the rapidly changing nature of knowledge (in virtually all fields), our daily intellectual improvement diet must include the freshest thinking within our professional domain. Becoming more skillful in interpersonal transactions is also a function of intellectual discipline. While not all of us are naturals at the interpersonal stuff, we can learn the skills necessary to work well with others. As well, we must become comfortable with NOT knowing. Actually, we can learn to leverage our ignorance to feed the desire for learning.

The late Stephen Covey noted in his 2004 book, *The 8th Habit*, that early in his life he felt absolutely ignorant. Covey describes being overwhelmed by all that he *didn't* know, feeling as if there was always a cloud of "ignorance" overshadowing what he *did* know. Consequently, he set out on a mission to overcome that umbrella of ignorance, by learning as much as he could. As that learning journey unfolded, the reality he found instead was that the more he learned, the more ignorant he felt.

Did he learn a lot in the process? You bet. But the main thing he learned was that the more we learn, the more there is to know.

PHYSICAL FITNESS

Body and Soul

Chopra (2009) describes five "breakthroughs," in relation to physical wellness:

1) Our physical bodies are fiction, more verb than noun.
2) Our bodies are conduits of energy.
3) Heightened awareness will put us in greater tune to the needs/health of our bodies.
4) We don't control our genes, but we have great power to determine which ones are turned on and which ones are turned off. Awareness is the vehicle of that power.
5) Time is our ally, not our enemy (but it's up to us to view it as such).

Those breakthroughs provide an excellent foundation for our discussion of physical fitness.

Energy

Leadership requires a disproportionately large amount of physical energy. It is significantly a brain thing. Our brains burn 20 percent of the energy we produce in our bodies, though they account for only about two percent of the body mass. Energy is required for decision-making because few consequential decisions can be relegated to automatic pilot. Duhigg (2012) speaks to the power habits play in our lives. Habits are, in effect, ways of conserving energy. When we relegate things to habit, we essentially are "greasing the skids" of our cognitive energy flow. Whenever we commit an act to habit (e.g., brushing our teeth, buttoning a shirt, commuting, saying "thank you"), we are reducing the amount of cognitive energy required to attend to that act. This automating of the routine frees mental energy for the more difficult tasks.

Energy matters a *lot* in challenging roles. We must learn to read our bodily rhythms and metabolism, to tune in to signs that our energy is flagging (e.g., restlessness, yawning, hunger, and difficulty concentrating). A lot of things impact our energy, and thus, our feelings, our image, and our effectiveness. Mercola (2015) notes five components that he believes have particularly negative impact in that regard: processed food, chemicals in our environment and food, antibiotics in medicine and food, inactivity, and lack of sleep.

One of the anti-intuitive realities of energy is that the more energy we burn, the more energy we have. The body seems to ramp up to meet our energy needs, provided we supply it with the necessary nutrition, exercise, and rest.

Exercise

The exercise industry generates billions of dollars around the world, particularly large sums in the United States. Programs, trainers, gyms, competitive events, and exercise equipment proliferate, for the sole purpose of helping us attain higher levels of physical fitness (and, of course, to produce profit for the vendors).

While we often think of exercise in terms of running, lifting weights, stretching, yoga, swimming, competing in sports, etc., exercise in its simplest (and perhaps most effective) form is grounded in the act of simple movement. Simply standing burns more calories than sitting. Thus, one of the most effective things we can do to engage in exercise (with consequent positive health benefit) is to stand up and move around. Endless exercise infomercials basically get the message right: If we'll move around, we'll be more physically fit. Each one promotes their own tool or device to help us start moving around, but the bottom line is the same. Move around to improve fitness. The more holistic the movement, the better.

Examples of simple exercise undertakings which we can do at work or home, include: using a stand-up desk, taking brief but frequent walkabout breaks, standing or walking while talking on the phone, walking around the room as we read.

To be sure, more intense exercise regimens can be adopted, which include the likes of weight training, aerobic exercise, high intensity exercising, fartlek running, etc. All are good (unless taken to debilitative extremes) and all can have a positive impact on our physical, emotional and cognitive wellbeing. Like so many other aspects of fitness (as noted repeatedly thus far), they are most effective when implemented as habits, embedded into our daily lives.

Sleep

For many who have leadership positions, rest is evasive. The weight of responsibility never seems to take a vacation. Even worse, the burdens attached to leadership often seem heaviest when we're trying desperately to get some sleep. It's almost as if sleep has to mercifully find us, rather than the other way around.

Several strategies can improve the likelihood of realizing much needed rest. Here are some ideas that have been used by others, with substantive results:

- Refraining from the use of digital screens like computers, smartphones, and televisions at least one hour prior to bedtime.
- Getting to bed earlier.
- Darkening our bedrooms COMPLETELY.
- Setting the room temperature cooler for sleeping purposes.
- Moving devices that emit magnetic fields and/or make use of LED lighting well away from our beds.

Sufficient sleep is critical to maintaining physical fitness. We simply cannot function optimally without it.

Poor Diet

For decades of my adult life I engaged in regular physical exercise (still do, for that matter). During almost all those years I told myself that one compelling reason to do so was that it allowed me to "eat whatever I wanted." And, eat I did. Sweets galore, soft drinks by the case, breads and pastas to no end. It probably doesn't say much for my intelligence that I continually struggled to manage my weight even though I was running miles on end and lifting weights regularly.

I wrote the insidious deteriorating physical conditions off to advancing age. Old guys are supposed to develop large girths, right? Middle-aged guys aren't supposed to be strong, are they? We're expected to get stiff and inflexible as we age, correct? Blood pressure issues come with age, don't they?

To ameliorate those presumed age-related physical diminishments I ate margarine instead of butter, used vegetable oils instead of natural fats, drank diet sodas instead of the sugared ones, and consumed every conceivable kind of "whole wheat" or "whole grain" product I could. I followed the standard line that a low fat diet was the way to fight off unwanted weight and diseases of the vessels (e.g., cardiovascular disease, diabetes, and hypertension).

I have since learned better. I was acting in direct opposition to my own best interests. The old saw of "you are what you eat" began to take on new significance for me. I was living in ignorance for most of those years, even though I was following the conventional dietary wisdom, which just happened to dovetail nicely with the marketing goals of food producers and marketers. My most recent learning about wellness and fitness (physical, intellectual, and emotional/spiritual) leads me to believe I was being sold, and was buying, a bill of goods that were simply NOT in my best interest. Rather, those approaches were, in fact, hastening me toward the vessel-hardening diseases.

Dr. Robert Lustig (2009) puts it this way, "No amount of exercise can overcome a poor diet."

80% Nutrition, 20% Exercise

Diets don't work, not for the long haul, anyway. My wife and I tried numerous diets over the years. When we would get to a point where we were carrying a few too many pounds or our clothes would feel a bit too snug, we would then embark on one diet or another in order to trim a few pounds. Most worked, for the short term. But most also fizzled, as they were either impractical, too expensive, took too much work, or simply didn't taste good. All the while, we continued to engage in exercise of one kind or another - walking, jogging, lifting weights, watching and mimicking video-exercise-maniacs of endless varieties.

Underlying our weight control efforts was the belief that with enough exercise we could "eat whatever we wanted." Turns out we were wrong. WAY wrong! The diets never worked for the long haul and the exercise, no matter how extreme, was never able to offset the effects of poor eating habits.

Thus, we began a journey in late 2012 that completely transformed the way we think and eat and feel and exercise and work. The impact on our body/mind/spirit wellness has been amazing.

Weight has melted off of us, and our bodies have become leaner. Our wellness markers have improved on all fronts (blood pressure, blood sugar, cognition, stamina, reduced inflammation in joints, reduced effects of arthritis, disappearance of the afternoon "sinking" phenomenon, etc.).

Are we starving ourselves? No way! We eat as much as we want and never count calories or limit volume in any way whatsoever. For the first time in my life, portions sizes are something I pay little attention to.

Here's a driving tenet of our newly found approach to wellness:

Our physical health is 80% what we eat, 20% exercise.

Consequence or Coincidence?

> "When diet is wrong medicine is of no use. When diet is correct medicine is of no need."
>
> -AYURVEDIC PROVERB

69

Physician and wellness advisor, Dr. Roby Mitchell (you can find him here: http://drfitt.com/), is fond of saying, "Consequence is no coincidence." Our habits guide our behavior, every day, in small ways and large. From our daily hygiene routines to the way we read the news to the order in which we eat our food to the processes we use to organize our schedules, all are driven by habits. In most cases, there's not a right or wrong way to do such things. For instance, there's not a correct way to shave our faces/legs, but each of us has a habitual process by which we accomplish the task.

Some habits, however, are far more consequential than a routine one like shaving. When it comes to our physical health, our spiritual state, our eating habits, our intellectual growth, our dispositions when interacting with others, our habits have far greater impact on our happiness, success, and wellbeing.

Can we change our habits? You bet! First, we have to want to. To be certain, "Consequence is no coincidence."

Inflammation

Inflammation is a monster that does our body great harm from the inside out. None of us would fire up an oxy-acetylene cutting torch and give our external bodies a nice "roasting," multiple times per day. Yet, we do that very thing to the inside of our bodies by eating sugars (in all their 50 plus name-states) and excessive carbohydrate-dense foods (i.e., grain-based and highly processed foods).

The cumulative harm done to our health via the incessant advance of inflammation manifests itself in various ways. According to Dr. Mark Hyman (2015), "These include allergies, arthritis, autoimmune diseases, fatigue, sinus problems, hormonal disorders, obesity, high blood pressure, cholesterol, digestive diseases like irritable bowel syndrome, reflux, and colitis, and even mood disorders like depression and anxiety — just to name a few."

Dr. Robert Lustig (2009) alludes to this slow-cooking effect on the inside of our bodies as the Maillard Reaction, which is the exact same phenomena of the browning of toast, the searing of a steak, or the golden-brown color of cooked French fries.   Only, inside of our bodies, this *searing* of the vessels is not such a good thing. Just as with the outside of the toast, steak, and potatoes mentioned above, the browning effect on our vessels represents a "hardening" that is quite unhealthy.

Dr. Roby Mitchell (2014) discusses how inflammation is, in effect, our body's attempt to wage war on what he calls "critters" that it deems to be invasive. Those "critters" are invaders that trigger our autoimmune system to respond with inflammation that is supposed to affect the demise of said critters. The bad news is that we continually "feed" the critters, through our eating choices, what they most want and need - high doses of sugars, via processed sugars, grains, and carbohycrate-dense products.

When we remove the stuff the "critters" like, we reduce the body's persistent response of "scorching" the "critters" with inflammation. This then mitigates the internal "cooking" of our bodies. (Lots of metaphors, huh?) Bottom line? We must quit killing/cooking ourselves from the inside out by choosing instead foods that the "critters" hate and our bodies love.

Time to turn off the torch!

Hammering the Dashboard

Gaining new insight into wellbeing, with respect to individual *and* organizational health, has been a critical part of my learning in recent years. One of the most profound nuggets of learning has been right under my nose the whole time. I was just too busy to notice it. That nugget? When we focus on treating symptoms we end up ignoring the root causes of illness, to our demise.

Most of us drive vehicles electronically equipped to activate the "check engine" light when something is amiss. While annoying, that "check engine" light is an alert, a warning, that there is something wrong "on the inside" that will eventually cause significant compromise to our car's performance (and probably cost us a lot of money, too). Not one of us would promptly take a hammer to the check engine light on the dashboard, in belief that if we simply eliminate the symptom the problem is solved.

Yet, that is exactly what we do so often with our individual and organizational health. We attack the symptoms, with drugs, with initiatives, with surgery, with new regulations, with _____ (you can fill in the blank). We can often temporarily make the symptoms go away. We have not, however, addressed the underlying causes of those symptoms. Unaddressed, those root causes will cost us a high price down the road if we choose to believe that, since the symptoms are temporarily gone, the problems have been cured.

Consider how that analogy applies to our personal health. And, consider how it applies to the health of the organizations/communities to which we lend our efforts. Drop the hammer, and move away from the dashboard.

Pasteboard Anyone?

I've heard the argument that it really doesn't matter what you eat as long as it's filling. Really? If that were the case, then by far the best and cheapest route would be to shred some pasteboard, sprinkle it with some salt and sugar, then eat to our heart's content. BUT WAIT! Much of our processed food is little more than that. We would never fuel our car with water and expect it to run well. Since our bodies are much more complex organisms than a car we can't expect to fuel them with food void of nutrition and achieve optimal performance.

So, what is real food? It's food that is in the form closest to what it looked like when harvested. It's food that is raised with zero or minimal chemical inputs (e.g., pesticides, herbicides, fungicides, antibiotics, hormones, etc.). It's food that hasn't been chemically injected, boxed, waxed, and/or colored. It's food that has been raised in healthy, living, vibrant soil.

Real, nutrient-dense food is essential if we want to live long and healthy lives, and if we intend to most effectively lead the organizations we serve.

Fitness for Service and Personal Greatness

Clayton Christensen (2012) notes that, because our minds are finite, we rely on aggregating data in order to make some kind of sense of it. We have to use trends, graphs, spreadsheets, and polls in order to digest and parse the voluminous amount of information with which we are confronted. Via that process we "keep score" on ourselves, and others.

Christensen posits that God, however, has an infinite mind, thus is not subservient to data aggregation in order to make sense of things. In effect, Christensen argues, God sees the whole, and does not need to slice and dice data in order to understand it. Neither does God have need to score us against one another.

What then are the implications for us, as we consider the meaning and impact of our lives? Our personal greatness does not and will not depend on salary made, titles achieved, trophies won, businesses started, books sold, elected offices held, widgets shipped, or customers satisfied.

Rather, our personal greatness is dependent on only two things:

1) How faithfully we have adhered to God's plan for our lives.
2) How well we have loved and served those who were placed within our sphere of influence (whether that number be one or one billion).

All else is inconsequential.

It is worth remembering that, as leaders, our personal greatness derives in no small degree from our holistic fitness, along all three dimensions – emotional/spiritual, intellectual, and physical. And, that has direct implications for the "greatness" of those who follow our lead.

4

Dealing with Ambiguity

"A leader is best when people barely know he exists, when his work is done, his aim fulfilled, they will say: we did it ourselves."

— LAO TZU

Ambiguity

Ambiguity and complexity are givens in the work of leadership. Unclear futures and unclear pathways toward those futures are about the only certainties. In a rapidly changing world, defining the problems may be more important than crafting the solutions. It is within that milieu that leaders and teams get a sense of the trends and can more accurately anticipate potential opportunities, successes, and failures. This does not imply a lack of integrity or lack of commitment to the mission. Rather, it implies an understanding that though the path forward may be uncertain, remaining stagnant is not an option.

Context is everything in leadership, and in the associated decision-making processes. Wise leaders garner varying perspectives to gain better understanding of the contexts. While seeking and obtaining myriad viewpoints, perspectives, and worldviews does not make the decisions any easier, it does make them more informed. Considering life's paradoxes and contradictions, the resulting ambiguity often drives us toward making "guesses." Informed decision-making is the act of making *educated* guesses.

Distortion

Dr. Gaylen Paulson at the University of Texas at Austin introduced me to an idea that has altered the way I think about the world. He notes that many of us use eyeglasses and/or contact lenses. Paulson asserts that in that process we choose to purposefully "distort" our vision. He says that we use these devices to cause us to see the world around us as we assume it *should* look, rather than the way it appears to us without the assistance of those devices. In effect, we have deliberately distorted our vision, based on some assumptions.

We often do the same thing with regard to our worldview. We view the world – its problems, its challenges, its politics, its religions – through lenses of our own choosing. These lenses through which we view the world, and the complexities of its social interplay, distort our vision. In effect, we make the world fit the assumptions and preconceptions we already have, and thus, its appearance fits our biases.

Perhaps we should consider the possibility that we deceive (or worse, limit) ourselves...

Filtered

We use filters all the time. We filter the oil in our cars, we filter water, we filter air via our heating/cooling systems, and we filter our coffee. Generally, filters serve a cleansing role, catching the "bad stuff" before it causes ill health or mechanical failure or bad taste.

We also employ the use of psychological filters, by which we screen data, experiences, even people. Like those physical filters mentioned above, our psychological filters are intended to protect us from stuff, people, thinking, and/

or behaviors that we deem detrimental, or at least, not what we prefer to embrace.

WARNING! We should "check" those psychological filters regularly to make sure they're not feeding some unrecognized prejudice, limiting our interactions to only those who look, think, or believe like we do, precluding us from learning from someone new (even if their hair is purple or they wear boots or they go to a different church than we do). We should not allow our "filters" to inhibit us from developing fully.

Filters are good, mostly; but only as long as they don't keep us from being all we can be and knowing all we can know.

Assumed Deficiency

Leaders in robust businesses and organizations *assume* that not all systems and processes are operating in peachy keen fashion. That's why they adopt an attitude of and commitment to continuous improvement. They understand clearly that, despite constant revision and polishing, inventories deplete unexpectedly, equipment fails, customer service falters, supply chains bottleneck, or performance metrics suffer. The list of "things to work on" goes on forever.

Even on our ranch, my wife and I have a never-ending list of things to patch, repair, replace, re-locate, re-build, or re-purpose. This quote by an old rancher really resonates with me: "If you can't find something to fix, you're not looking hard enough." Exactly!

Thus, it matters not what kind of organization or endeavor we are involved in, attention to continuous improvement must be an assumed mindset. It's not about blaming someone for failures or malfunctions. It's not about finding fault. It's not about cursing conditions or circumstances. It's about getting up everyday and heading to the office, pasture, classroom, or shop floor with the intention of getting better, every day, on purpose.

Sticky Problems

Sticky problems are the ones that seem to defy solutions. They're the ones that won't go away, or that seem to grow under their own steam, or that have the innate ability to evolve into new and different iterations each time we seem to get a handle on them.

That last dynamic, in fact, is quite telling. Complex problems are the result of complex dealings among and between complex people. Most all the variables are complex, and most all the interactions are complex. Thus, the problems are confounding, with the solutions being elusive and fleeting.

If we look for a solution that will finally put a problem to rest *forever*, we deceive ourselves. The solutions to complex problems must be at least as malleable and evolutionary as the problems themselves. Just like those superbugs that tend to evolve faster than the drugs or pesticides we invent to kill them, those sticky kinds of problems are not going away, and they are certainly not going to be fixed easily and permanently.

All things considered, the best course of action in dealing with those sticky and evolving problems is to *LEARN* -

    learn what worked last time,
    learn about what others are trying,
    learn about the root causes of the problem,
    learn how to attack the problem from a different angle,

LEARN,

    LEARN,

        LEARN!

Gardner (1990) states, "Leadership is not tidy. Decisions are made and then revised or reversed. Misunderstandings are frequent, inconsistency inevitable.

Achieving a goal may simply make the next goal more urgent: inside every solution are the seeds of new problems." (p. 22)

Bad Things

A few years ago I encountered one of the young men I coached several decades earlier (I'll call him Gabe). We had had no communications since his high school graduation. As Gabe and I reminisced about "the good old days" we recalled a number of the games and experiences we shared in the football arena. We might have even added a few embellishments to the remembered facts. As well, we caught up on each other's lives since he had graduated. Gabe had gotten married, become a father, and was doing quite well for himself in the profession he had chosen. His evident success and happiness made me proud.

Gabe told me that he had relied often on one of the "speeches" I gave in those tense pre-game moments before a team heads onto the field. My mind quickly rushed back over the numerous admonitions and encouragements I would deliver in those moments of pre-game closeness (one of my favorite parts of coaching was the "brotherhood" involved). I was never sure if the players heard any of my blatherings just before kickoff. With a bit of apprehension, I asked Gabe which "speech" he was referencing.

Gabe fixed his eyes firmly on mine and reminded me of my oft-delivered counsel to the young men and women I coached. It went something like this: "Bad things are doubtless gonna happen tonight, to both teams. The team that emerges victorious will not be the team that escapes adversity. The team that most effectively responds to the bad things will be successful in the end."

I can't tell you where I first heard those words (it might have been *my* high school football coach), but they obviously resonated with me. In fact, now that I've spent almost six decades in the unpredictable and sometimes turbulent waters of life, those words ring truer now than ever.

Bad stuff is gonna happen. Bad stuff is completely impersonal. Bad stuff doesn't discriminate. It happens to all of us. Life is not so much about avoiding bad stuff as it is about learning from it. Our experiences and what we learn from them are the things that ultimately define our lives. Our experiences (with family, with friends, with antagonists, with events) cause automatic neural mapping to occur in our brains; we call it memory. Life isn't fair; it doses out a good bit of bad stuff to all of us. The only choice we get in the matter is how we react to it, and what we learn from it.

Thanks, Gabe, for remembering, and for the memory.

Uncharted

Margaret Wheatley (2006) says, "The organizational chart never charts the organization." Organizations always resemble a cobbling together of partnerships rather than a tight chain of command. A better graphic to conceptualize these relationships is a web of interconnectivity.

Still, many leaders try to insist that the organizational chart rules, and the chain of command is the Holy Grail. The illusory idea here is that of CONTROL. When "permission" is required to work its way up, then back down, an elaborate command structure, then positive action, positive growth, and positive results are pretty much NOT guaranteed.

Here are some indicators of high performing organizations:

- Employees throughout the organization grasp the vision and can see their role within that concept.
- Employees are entrusted with the autonomy to make decisions within their purview, with the assumption and expectation that they will

make those decisions in alignment with the organization's driving principles (not check-off boxes).

- Significant resources are invested in the education (not just training) of employees along a broad range of skills, all in the interest of enhancing professional and personal growth.
- Information flows openly and freely in all directions throughout the web. There are NO SECRETS that are kept from others in the organization.
- Leaders in the organization spend the lion's share of their time teaching, talking, promoting, and praising efforts aligned to those driving principles.

Sound like a place you'd like to work?

Water Treading

We sometimes find ourselves treading water, either as individuals or as organizations. Usually, we tread water (metaphorically speaking) to stall for time, to rest a bit, or to survive in overwhelming conditions. We want or need to do *something* that will keep us afloat until we've decided on a course of action, or until someone comes along to rescue us. However, water treading as standard operating procedure is not in our best interest (either individually or organizationally). It's not a viable way of being. It consumes energy and gets us nowhere. It keeps us focused inwardly rather than outwardly.

Far better it is to pick a direction (*some* direction) and start swimming. Once we've started, we can monitor and adjust as conditions and circumstances dictate. At least we are headed somewhere, making some kind of progress, and gauging that progress against our goals (which can then be modified as needed).

Finally, water treading makes us easy targets - both from above the surface and below. That's probably *not* part of our strategic plan.

Ain't Nobody Dying Here

I once served with an assistant principal who saliently captured an excellent standard for "emergency" response. When others would be "on fire" about some current catastrophe – bells not working, buses being late, a food fight in the cafeteria, a malfunctioning fire alarm – this assistant principal regularly brought the team back to reality with a phrase we had heard from him a million times: "Hey, there ain't nobody dying here." He had a way of helping us sift through the clutter of urgency and the perceived level of emergency by framing it against a REAL barometer of alarm – life-threatening situations.

Whatever our workplace, there are always perceived "emergencies" – late shipments, phone systems that don't work, spilled milk, flat tires, rain when we need to be planting, etc. Almost all of those "emergencies" are best dealt with in a calm, reasonable, and attentive fashion, without panic.

I once read that emergency room physicians are taught to respond to all emergencies in a leisurely fashion. Observing those doctors in that environment sure seems to confirm that assertion. There is a reason those physicians don't panic – it never improves (and almost always worsens) the effectiveness of response. (And those folks frequently *ARE* dealing with life-threatening situations.) Reacting to adversity in a measured and judicious way (without panic) is a learnable skill. We can begin that learning NOW (especially if being "on fire" doesn't seem to be working for us).

Short Menu, Ugly Options

One of the first and most profound lessons folks learn as they move into leadership positions is about the constraints of decision-making. Monday morning quarterbacks are quite fond of second guessing leaders on the difficult decisions they make. That critiquing is often accompanied by the preface of, "Well, if it were me, I would..."

The reality is this: The decisions that most often present themselves to those in leadership positions are the difficult, ambiguous, and complex ones. Other folks in the organization readily make the decisions that are easy and low-risk. The tough decisions, the politically risky ones, the ones that have the look, smell, and feel of dilemma, most often get "kicked up the food chain."

Thus, when it's time to make those tough decisions, the menu of remaining options is almost always short and almost always ugly. The higher up the leadership ladder we get, the shorter and uglier the options become. And more often than not, those options are steeped in ambiguity.

Flat World

There was a time when…

- Three television networks owned the airwaves.
- Aspiring musicians had to get "discovered" and promoted.
- Print media controlled the news.
- A few publishers decided what got read, and who would write it.
- Select universities cornered the "talent" market.
- Your innovative product had to be vetted and blessed by some cadre of "experts."
- You couldn't access the world's marketplace or attention without someone else's permission.
- To be successful, you almost *had* to have connections.

No more. Now we can find whatever it is we're looking for, almost instantly. We can learn from whomever we want. We can acquire whatever information we seek. We can produce, write, play, build, and share whatever we decide to. We can do all those things without asking anyone's permission.

It is now a VERY FLAT WORLD. Friedman (2005) articulates this in irrefutable fashion. Gone are all those gatekeepers and barriers. Gone also is the safety of excuse making. No one can hold you back………but you.

Whatcha wanna be? Whatcha wanna do? Whatcha waiting for?

Dealing With Change

Change introduces much ambiguity. Change is a product of evolution, much more than one of revolution. Even though change is constantly coming our way, most folks are reticent about change (and many even resist it stridently).

So, what is the leader's role in managing change (either externally imposed or internally adopted)? Leaders can help by communicating clearly the need for change, while acknowledging the fear of it. That communication must be continual, and conducted through many media. A fundamental component of that communication is that successful people and successful organizations are the ones that are change adept, not change inept. Another critical message leaders can and should send is that change is best navigated through a mindset of continual improvement. In effect, the assimilation of change becomes assumed as a function of simply getting better and improving daily.

Leaders can also help in the assimilation of change by simplifying it is much as possible. Clear and concise language, tight and clean processes, open and transparent feedback loops, all help in the process of adapting to change. While both change and resistance to change are problematic, wise leaders can help reduce the anxiety.

To be certain, change is a bit unsettling, but being irrelevant is even more unsettling.

Change Prognosis

I frequently field questions from folks who'd like to "get their boss to change." Sadly, I can't help on this one and here's why. Either or both of the following conditions must be met in order for a person, a group, or an organization to significantly change their thinking and/or behavior:

- Circumstances are such that the person/group/organization has no alternative other than to seek a change in thinking/behavior in order to sustain their existence.

- A person/group/organization comes under a deep and powerful conviction that, in order to be all that they want to be, a change in thinking/behavior must occur.

The prognosis for change hinges upon two elements:

1) The person/group/organization must possess significant cognitive acumen (either personally or collectively).
2) The commitment to change must be extraordinarily powerful, powerful enough to compel substantive revision in the habits embedded in the daily fabric of their lives.

Externally forced change rarely works (history as my witness). Intrinsically driven change is doable but difficult (as noted above). The good news is that impassioned leaders with a powerful vision stand a decent chance of "pulling" others toward meaningful change (per the conditions noted above). First, however, those leaders must see the need and meet the conditions necessary, themselves.

Change Impediments

Change ain't easy, but it's one of the surest constants in life. Our bodies change, our thinking changes, the weather changes, economic conditions change, relationships change, cultures change.

Here are just some of the reasons many of us resist change:

- We're comfortable and happy right where/how we are, thank you!
- We're afraid of what lies on the other side of change.
- It just takes too much energy to change.
- If we're being successful in the current state, why change?
- We tried change once (or 50 times) before, and it just didn't work out.

These impediments to change often spring from the fact that we misperceive the constancy of change. It's sort of like the misperception of stillness.

We may *feel* like we're being still, when in fact we're on a planet that is spinning at approximately 1,000 miles per hour. And, Earth is hurtling around the sun at a speed of almost 19 miles per second. Finally, the entire Solar System is flying through space at a speed of 514,000 miles per hour. *Stillness* is a gross misperception and misrepresentation of the reality that exists. The same sort of psychological misperception is at play regarding change.

When we come to think of change as a constant to which we must adapt, we take a completely different view of it. Change happens to us (and our organizations) whether we like or not. The only question is how adept we are at adapting to it.

Paradox Dance

In leadership and in life we are constantly confronted with the presence of paradox. According to Morgan (1998) we are continually pushed-pulled in two different directions by bosses, by politics, by circumstances, by regulatory entities, by our values. It looks something like this:

Innovate	←------→	Avoid Mistakes
Think long term	←------→	Deliver results now
Cut costs	←------→	Increase morale
Reduce staff	←------→	Improve teamwork
Be flexible	←------→	Respect the rules
Collaborate	←------→	Compete
Decentralize	←------→	Retain control
Specialize	←------→	Be opportunistic
Low costs	←------→	High quality

Fisher, Ury, and Patton (1991) add to the list of paradoxes:

Form	←-----→	Substance
Economic considerations	←-----→	Political considerations
Internal considerations	←-----→	External considerations
Symbolic considerations	←-----→	Practical considerations
Immediate future	←-----→	Distant future
Ad hoc results	←-----→	The relationship
Hardware	←-----→	Ideology
Progress	←-----→	Respect for tradition
Precedent	←-----→	This case
Prestige/reputation	←-----→	Results
Political points	←-----→	Group welfare

To muddy the water even more, Bolman and Deal (1991) add their two cents' worth:

Group	←-----→	Overlaps
Differentiation	←-----→	Integration
Underuse	←-----→	Overload
Lack of clarity	←-----→	Lack of creativity
Excessive autonomy	←-----→	Excessive interdependence
Too loose	←-----→	Too tight
Authority	←-----→	Overcentralization
Goal-less	←-----→	Goal-bound
Irresponsible	←-----→	Unresponsive

Each goal of those dichotomous continua has merit. Yet, whenever we narrow our view of life/work/relationships/problems by thinking of them in isolated constructs (as shown above) we have, in effect, "simplified" the metrics. But life/work/relationships/problems defy simplified metrics; they must be considered and navigated holistically. It requires us to do the dance of paradox, to find the "sweet spot" on each continuum, but considered within the context of the whole.

The "sweet spot" on each of those continua above is found by viewing them through the lenses of our values, our ethical anchors. Nobody can determine our values and ethical anchors for us – that comes from thoughtful soul-searching and self-reflection. Wise mentors, great thinkers, and exemplars can all help us find our moral grounding, but at the end of the day, it's a learning journey we must take for ourselves. And, that journey never ends.

Authority's Paradox

A paradox of authority is that the more of it we have, the greater the temptation to insulate ourselves from feedback. To be sure, with authority comes responsibility, usually a LOT of responsibility. Time begins to feel like a constraint rather than an opportunity. So, we begin shielding ourselves from the very people and information and feedback we most need.

To resist the Authority Paradox, here are some helpful habits leaders can build into our lives/work:

- Ask questions directly of the customers/students/front-line employees frequently, and *LISTEN* to their responses.
- Walk the buildings. Make regular, on-site visits to see how the work is going, and the fidelity with which it is being conducted.
- Admit it when we don't know. Then, find out what we "don't know," and follow up by getting back to the person(s) who prompted our don't-know-moment in the first place.
- Make it safe for others to dissent, to debate, to disagree, to dialogue. Otherwise, we'll always and only get sugarcoated versions of truth.

- Stay focused on the individual development of *each* team member. Organizational improvement will follow.
- *ALWAYS* thank others - for their time, for their effort, for their thinking, for their feedback.

Creating a protective shield from critical feedback is like decorating our own prison cell, and getting comfortable in those trappings.

Certainty

Certainty implies there is no doubt, it's a done deal, can't miss, or guaranteed results. From a leadership perspective, certainty comes in two varieties: Outcome-based certainty and Purpose-based certainty.

Leaders who operate from an outcome-based certainty profess to know exactly the products and procedures they want delivered. No questions asked, no deviations. Bombast and mandate are two of their fundamental leadership tools. Dubious metrics and nonsensical protocols are common characteristics of organizations with this kind of leader. Folks working under leadership of this stripe find themselves in an environment in which standardization and homogeneity are the norm. Standards are set, outcomes are demanded, and deliverables required. Organizations under this kind of leadership manifest some interesting characteristics: "Hiding" is an asset, avoidance of responsibility is a life-extender, risk aversion improves chances of advancement, and blame-throwing is an art.

On the other hand...

Leaders who operate from a purpose-based certainty deftly articulate a vision of organizational pursuit and achievement that is worthy. Usually, this vision has been collectively crafted. These leaders display intense passion around and invest great personal energy in that vision. They create a permeating tapestry of relationships, resources, messages, and engagement around that vision, which is embedded into the day-to-day work of the organization.

Interconnectedness and interdependence are the valued hallmarks of the organizations led by this kind of leader. Folks who work with these leaders find themselves in an environment in which *mastery*, not standardization, is incentivized. They prosper in a climate of autonomy, in which the pathway toward the vision is malleable, customizable, and personalized. The incentives are most certainly there, though more symbolic, affective, and self-actualizing than tangible. It is a magical combination of both form and substance.

As leaders, we can and DO promote one type of certainty or the other. Is it the type we intend?

Control's Locus

Things we can control: Our attitude, our attention, our behavior/responses/reactions, the way we spend our time, what we choose to learn (or not), how we focus our resources (tangible and intangible), etc.

Things we can't control: The weather, what others think, how others act, how others expend their resources (tangible and intangible), etc.

There is little to be gained by squandering energy on things that are beyond our locus of control. And, MUCH to be gained by focusing on the things we *can* control.

Solutions Versus Answers

There seem to be some fundamental differences between solutions and answers.

Answers imply that...

- The knowledge already exists.
- Others have already figured it out.
- This problem is identical to many others.

- There is at least someone who has already found the combination.
- They can be found in a book (or on the internet).

Solutions imply that...

- Crafting is required.
- Previous solutions can help, but only tangentially.
- This problem is unique and nuanced.
- Leveraging, but not cloning, knowledge/skills from outside the field might be helpful.
- Synthesis, innovation, and collaboration are required.

Answers are handy to have, but they are have-able. Solutions are elusive and ghostlike. Having answers gives us closure. Seeking solutions gives us purpose. Answers can be begged, borrowed, or stolen. Solutions are creations. Answers represent learning in the past tense. Solutions require continued learning.

Hapkido

Hapkido is one version of the martial arts. As such, it is an approach to self-defense. Hapkido leverages the redirecting of force and the skillful use of circular rather than linear motion in order to subdue one's aggressor. Hapkido practitioners use skillful body positioning and the redirecting of force to avoid head-on, strength-versus-strength conflict.

As with the properties of water, Hapkido practitioners seek to go fluidly around, through, or over the object/aggressor. They attempt to circle or circumvent typical force-on-force conflict, which generally results in significant trauma/stress/damage to both parties.

Taking these concepts together, we can learn to deflect, redirect, circle around, blend, and merge the aggressive force of another aimed at us, leveraging it toward our own protection. Almost always, these concepts are considered within the context of self-defense from physical attack. In effect, Hapkido is the co-opting of the energy of the aggressor to achieve one's own defense/protection/ends. Note also that its application is NOT intended to destroy the other.

Now consider the possible use of the Hapkido concepts of self-defense described above when being aggressed by others in intellectual and/or emotional ways. We can also learn to effectively manage interpersonal conflict in those contexts by deflecting, redirecting, flowing around, and co-opting the aggressive force of another, and thus, overcoming it. And we can achieve those ends without the force-on-force carnage.

As do the practitioners of Hapkido, we can only deploy and refine such skills through our full attention, discipline and purposeful practice.

Resistance

Resistance is the phenomena of holding something back. Ways it manifests itself are through non-compliance, through argument, through diversion, through lack of acceptance, or even through downright defiance or hostility.

I have seen resistance to my efforts/thinking as a family member, as a church member, as a faculty member, as a teacher, as a coach, as a principal, as a professor, as a superintendent, and as a rancher (yep, even from animals). I suspect you have encountered resistance, too, in one form or another.

What might be some useful strategies in dealing with resistance? Here are a few:

- Consider the possibility that my goal/objective/directive is actually wrong or fool hardy.
- Consider the possibility that I have not communicated clearly. Have I been as clear about the "why" as I have about the "what" and the

"how"? If others don't know or understand the "why," it's probably not happening.

- Consider the possibility that I failed to invite others into the decision (when time and the nature of the situation allows). Did I garner and consider many perspectives before moving ahead with my resistance-creating decision?
- Consider the possibility that fear or discomfort or lack of confidence or loss (of some kind) is the catalyst for the resistance I am experiencing. Knowing that these phenomena are common resistance generators, have I painted a clear picture about the risks and benefits to be anticipated?
- Consider the possibility that the resistance comes from suspicions about my motives. Have I articulated well the fact that pursuit of a particular goal is about *US*, not about me? Either consciously or subconsciously, others are assessing my motives. It is wise for me to thoroughly go through the same process.

The effectiveness of leaders (in whatever role) and the enthusiasm of followers (in whatever form) depend greatly on the ability to anticipate and deal with resistance.

Conflict's Derivatives

Conflict happens! It occurs in every organizational arrangement and every relationship. Depending on how we manage the conflict, the results can range from total catastrophe to cathartic experience (and everything in between). Conflict managed in an unhealthy manner causes personal anxiety, creates barriers to success, and tears down relationships. Unhealthy conflict is based on one side or the other "winning" or diminishing the other party. Well-managed conflict, on the other hand, moves us fluidly toward our goals and makes relationships stronger. It is centered on understanding, empathy, clarity, and seeking a better-than-the-present solution.

There is a range of possibilities by which we can handle conflict, shown below.

- :-) **Integrating** - A "third way" is sought by which all parties are affirmed/satisfied.
- :-) **Compromising** - Each side wins a little, each side loses a little.
- :(**Dominating** - Power is used to impose one's will on another.
- :(**Obliging** - Giving in to the other person/group.
- :(**Avoiding** - Play like it's not happening.

As is the case in most life-issues, we get to choose how we deal with conflict. And, since there is always the "other" involved in conflict, we have to be aware of how they are approaching and dealing with the conflict as well. Interestingly, we get to approach each conflict situation as an independent/unique event; thus, we have to make a conscious decision about how we will handle it with each new occurrence.

At the end of the day, our personal health and wellbeing is dependent on how satisfied we are at the resolution of the conflict. Same goes for the "other."

Walking in Stupid

Lack of knowledge, or worse yet, self-chosen ignorance, is a looming barrier to our success in life and in work. A far bigger danger to us than ignorance (of either variety) is the illusion of knowledge. When we face challenges, deal with problems, and enter conversations assuming that we know plenty, we have created subtle cognitive constraints that limit our acquisition of new knowledge.

We can learn to inculcate curiosity within our own minds, but it takes some discipline. Achieving the beginner's mind is even more difficult if we succumb to the perception of urgency. Urgency, real or imagined, almost always narrows our focus and limits our openness to possibilities that lie in the periphery of our consciousness.

In the book *Mavericks at Work*, Taylor and Labarre (2008) reported the results of studying the leaders of organizations that have experienced phenomenal success in the advent of the digital age. They quote one of those leaders directly: "Whatever day it is, something in the world changed overnight, and you better figure out what it is and what it means. You have to forget what you just did and what you just learned. You have to walk in stupid every day."

Hope's Replacement

I once worked for a chief executive who pushed my thinking and performance in a lot of ways (I'll call him Ben). Ben was a classic visionary – it seemed his eyes were always on the horizon. He was constantly pulling those of us on his team to higher levels of performance, using every tool at his disposal.

One of the things Ben taught me was to (try to) eliminate the use of the word "hope" from my professional vocabulary. Ben insisted that when we use "hope" as a verb in articulating the aspirations of our organization (whether at the micro level, or at the macro level) it implies an element of victimhood. It is almost as if the realization of our espoused goals is at the complete mercy of circumstances. To be sure, there are a LOT of things beyond our control, especially when it comes to accomplishing worthy goals in a complex organizational environment. However, when we say we "hope" for one outcome or another as a result of money/time/effort invested in a particular strategy or project, it is almost as if we are creating excuses (or at least a defensible "out") for the failure of that strategy or project.

What verb should we use in place of "hope"? Several suggested replacement verbs work: Intend, Plan, Expect, Aim, or Anticipate. While all are suitable synonyms for the word "hope," each one implies that the actor has a more powerful role in making the desired outcome a reality.

I have been purposefully replacing the word "hope" with one of those other verbs for around 10 years now. To this day, I will slip and use it accidentally. It's harder to eliminate than you think. I *intend* to improve my performance in that regard.

Kicking the Marshmallow

Affecting organizational improvement is extremely difficult. Implementing some kind of lasting change in an organization is akin to kicking a marshmallow. Not just any marshmallow, though. Imagine a monster marshmallow, measuring 10 feet high and 10 feet in diameter. One can back off and take a full-steam run at such a marshmallow and kick it with all your might. The result would be a fairly significant dent in the marshmallow. Thus, the "change" has been duly imposed.

Immediately, however, the marshmallow begins to recover its previous shape, slowly but surely fluffing back out to its original form.

Such is the way of most attempts at externally imposed "change" or "reform" on organizations. While the organization (i.e., team, family, school, government, business, etc.) seems compliant to the initial attempt at change, its ingredients and texture somehow seem to conspire to return to its pre-reformed state.

I've lived that kicking-the-marshmallow experience several times, with similar results.

Nimbleness

Growth - in plants, in animals, in humans, in learning - NEVER follows a straight line. It occurs in fits and starts, ups and downs, sprints and diversions.

Why then do we assume that we can craft stability in an organization by pre-defining its movements, its plans, its trajectory? If nothing else, we should read, and learn, from history. Those that are adept at adapting win the day – and the profit, and the customers, and the satisfaction of a job well done, and the future, and happiness.

How might we make nimbleness an assumption in our organization, rather than some aspiration? For starters, we must begin to get comfortable with the pervasiveness of ambiguity, paradoxes and contradictions.

5

Eyes on the Horizon: Vision

"The greatest danger for most of us is not that our aim is too high and we miss it, but that it is too low and we reach it."

- MICHELANGELO

Vision and Purpose

Our minds hold dreams for the future and memories of the past. We live on the demarcation line between the two. None of us knows what the future holds, but for those who don't consider the possibilities, every day is a startling surprise. Such folks are in constant reaction mode. Those of us who lead others are compelled, both morally and pragmatically, to engage the community we lead in crafting a vision of "where we want to go." Passion must inhabit the vision and that vision must be perceived to be inclusive by all.

Somehow, we must work to shape the vision of our organizations to a higher aspiration than simply improving the bottom line or making the best widget on the planet. In consulting with the leadership team of a very successful screen-printing company, I engaged them in dialogue about how much more powerful it is to view their work as helping others express their pride and support for a cause than to simply view their job as smearing paint on articles of clothing. What they "do" for a living can be thought of as simply painting cloth and selling it, or it can be thought of as helping people and organizations express themselves. Which is the better vision?

Vision implies purpose. Considering carefully the purpose of our existence, both as individuals and as organizations is critical. Purpose matters a lot. Our vision must always center on the greater good (not just profit) and a better future.

Audacity

Be audacious in crafting a vision that inspires and compels others to join in the quest. Dream boldly, even audaciously. Bland and uninspiring vision makes for bland and uninspiring pursuit of that vision. Aim unabashedly and unashamedly for the extraordinary. Block (2008) reminds us, "Advice, recommendations, and obvious actions are exactly what increase the likelihood that tomorrow will be just like yesterday." (p. 109)

Because the world is an integrated and interwoven milieu of systems (and sub-systems), any vision for a particular organization must attend to how it is situated in the overall contexts. Our vision must be a compelling conceptual construct. All members of the organization must easily see how they fit into the big picture and readily understand how they can contribute in concrete ways to the pursuit of that vision.

Effective leaders understand that the visioning process is a little like being in fog: You can see clearly that which is right in front of you, but not at all that which is beyond (whether it be catastrophe or opportunity).

We must not confuse vision with a list of actions. Outcomes are the evidence of movement toward our vision, and the processes that depict that movement should be negotiable and malleable. The strategic plans and the mission action steps take us toward the vision. They are the "how" of getting to the "where" that the vision establishes.

While many variables and factors determine the success, even the survival, of an organization, history clearly details for us the following: Those clans, tribes, chiefdoms, states, and nations that have been led by forward-looking leaders have been the ones that have best weathered the inevitable challenges and threats to their existence. Often, it has proven to be the fact that those visionary leaders were best at understanding and leveraging the power of resource and technological development. What happens to far too many leaders is that they get mired in the mundane, trapped in the trivial, and thus never raise their eyes (and their thinking) to the horizon.

While developing a vision for the organization is inherently a political process, we must not let the politics of the process become a more powerful message than the vision itself. The distillation and dissemination of vision serves to embed and perpetuate values. Over time, depending on the deliberateness of the dissemination, organizational members who cannot abide those values tend to leave. If the dissemination process is not thorough, then members who do not share the values tend to stay in the organization, and thus, dilute the values and the vision.

Vision statements should be pithy, focused, succinct, and simple enough for all to understand. From the leader's perspective, our collective vision must become a mantra. We must communicate that vision in a thousand ways and across all stakeholders. Our eyes have to constantly move to the horizon, even as we attend to the trail in front of us.

Busyness
We get pretty busy doing "stuff." We invest tons of our time, money, labor, and energy into making stuff happen.

A valued friend and colleague recently referred to some of his father's guidance to him as a young man. His dad taught him that you could tell what was important to a person by watching three things: 1) How they spend their time, 2) How they spend their energy, and 3) How they spend their money.

It is rather important for us to think carefully about what it is we get so busy doing, what we invest ourselves in. The best stuff – things like friendship, faithfulness, love, and meaningful relationships – is built over time, powered by our constant attention and personal investment.

Marvelous are the results when our busyness is tightly aligned to and synchronized with our business. When that dynamic exists, some pretty cool "stuff" results.

Messy Work
Leadership is not for sissies.

While many look enviously at those in leadership positions, they rarely understand the kinds of issues that leaders are usually trying to resolve. The list of challenges that require the best of leaders includes:

- Dealing with special interests (which *always* have an agenda),
- Discerning and mitigating the contaminants of team chemistry and productivity,
- Finding and wisely allocating precious resources,
- Predicting the future in relation to the organization, and
- Crafting adaptive measures in response to those futures.

None of those challenges come in the form of multiple-choice tests. And, all of them are fraught with political, organizational, and financial implications.

The best leaders I know are VERY aware that leadership is a collective process, not a singular undertaking. The best leaders I know interact often and meaningfully with folks in every nook and cranny of the organization, constantly probing for feedback, data, and ideas for improvement. They speak often and well of the organizational members who invest themselves with gusto in the work of the organization. And, they focus their eyes, their ears, their words, their thoughts, and their hearts on the BIG mission drivers of the organization. (And consequently, help others do the same).

The late Stephen Covey phrased it beautifully: "The main thing is to keep the Main Thing the MAIN THING." Amen!

Clarity

Clarity results when we...

- Think often and deeply about our principles/values.
- Come up against what are obviously life-impacting decisions.
- Fail at something important.
- Succeed at something important.
- Are pressed to reflection by a valued mentor.
- Have a scrape with death (our own or that of a loved one).

Clarity evades us when we...

- Are too busy to *THINK*.
- Forsake or forget our values.
- Spend too much time/effort on the mundane.
- Neglect our loved ones.
- Lose sight of the "main thing."

Life is better when we view and live it with clarity. And that view is completely within our control.

7th Unborn Generation

I read several years ago that, historically, many of the Native American tribes used a collaborative process by which to govern themselves. Though the structures of those ruling councils and their constitutions varied, many operated by a set of guiding principles that premised decisions on ecological sustainability.

One of those commonly accepted principles was this: Always make decisions with the seventh unborn generation in mind.

Oren Lyons, Chief of the Onondaga Nation, is quoted as follows: "We are looking ahead, as is one of the first mandates given us as chiefs, to make sure and to make every decision that we make relate to the welfare and well-being of the seventh generation to come. . . ."

What about the seventh generation to come? Where are we taking them? What will they have? Thinking in terms of the wellbeing of our descendants alters the urgency we feel in decision-making, and it brands those decisions with the wisdom of sustainability. If we take the long view of sustainability in our daily decision-making, how might our organizations, our communities, our "tribes" and our families benefit?

Traction

If what we are selling as vision doesn't resonate, then it's not a worthy vision.

There are many reasons a vision fails to get traction. It might be bland, generic, odorless, confusing, lifeless, wimpy, or any other reason that doesn't move us, compel us to action, stimulate our energy, or attract our effort.

Visioning for the future is best done through inquiry, dialogue, debate, and collective wisdom. Through discussing aspirations, dreams, wishes, and intentions a vision begins to form organically. When that process occurs, the resulting vision is one that captures the aspirations of all and embraces the commitment of all.

True vision focuses the attention and investment of virtually all members of a group or organization. They adopt it and pursue it because they find it meaningful and worthy, not because it appears on the company letterhead and website. Each team member is able see how they can contribute in the pursuit of that vision, in specific and concrete ways.

If the vision for our organization does not do that, then it's probably time to re-assess and recalibrate. The starting point is to be constantly having consequential conversations about the future we imagine for our organization.

Settling

Too often we settle for the best from a menu of bad options. Sometimes we have little choice in the matter. For instance, as a junior high student I *might* have gotten into some kind of trouble (no fault of my own, of course). The assistant principal *might* have responded by giving me a choice of going to In-School-Suspension or receiving swats with a paddle (yes, that still happened when I was in school). Clearly, my options in that scenario were ugly and few. Life sometimes presents itself in that ugly-set-of-options format.

However, situations like that are more rare than we tend to believe. Predominantly we have a world of options available to us, if we just take the time to consider them. When thinking about our aspirations for our families and organizations – our VISION for the future – there is no need to settle for a best-of-the-worst list of options. We can dream big. We can aim high. And we should.

When skeptics and naysayers question such an approach, we can respond with these kinds of questions:

Why would we invest our time, effort, resources, and lives pursuing the status quo?

Why would we wish for and work for any less?
Why would we aim at mediocrity?
Why would we *settle*?

Past and Future

We perpetually stand astraddle the threshold between the past and the future. The past is important, but not nearly as important as the future.

The past is for reference;
> the future is for preference.

The past represents energy spent;
> the future represents energy potentials.

The past stores old memories/experiences;
> the future offers endless possibilities for new versions of both.

The past harbors a few regrets (or a lot);
> the future only the opportunity to reduce or avoid them.

The past is the haven of the powerful influences that shaped us;
> the future possesses our own acts of shaping.

The past was the path of our previous learning;
> the future offers a highway to new knowledge, skills, and ways of thinking.

> We do well to focus our attention forward instead of rearward.

Vibrant Futures

If we want vibrant futures for families and organizations, there are a few Dos and Don'ts to consider.

Things we *should* do:

- Be open-minded in the visioning process. Think big and encourage others to do so, too.
- Gain a wide range of perspectives (both from within and outside of our field).
- Acknowledge and value the gifts and talents others on the team bring to the table.
- Take time to metabolize information.
- Understand that emotion and personal dispositions almost always trump empirical data as rationale for action (or inaction). We should frame positions and messages accordingly.
- Approach problems and people with a curious mind, through skillful inquiry.

Things we *shouldn't* do:

- Try to convince others they're wrong. It's a waste of time and energy.
- Explain stuff ad infinitum.
- Embarrass or humiliate others.
- Ruin a good plan by over-bureaucratizing it (with too many rules/procedures/protocols/restrictions).
- Put all our eggs in one basket. Bold and risky ventures are best rolled out as pilot programs.
- Make hasty assumptions about outcomes or people. Both tend to defy prediction.

There are no guarantees, but better futures are more likely to emerge when we attend well to this prescription.

Storytelling

Storytelling took a bad rap when I was growing up. My parents had a pretty dim view of my brothers and me if they ever caught us "telling a story" (i.e., lying).

Turns out storytelling may not always be such a bad thing. Truthful stories are just fine and actually need to be told. The fact is, our story *will* be told. We can tell it for ourselves or we can let others tell it for us. We can define ourselves, or be defined.

Our story gets told through our intentions, through our habits, through our gestures, through our service, through our acts, through our interactions with others, and, occasionally, even through our words.

If we're gonna be the storyteller, it is imperative that we know what story we want to tell.

Let Go Them Chains

Viewing life through the windshield instead of the rearview mirror is the healthiest way to live.

There is no value in carrying our burdens around with us every minute of every day. Perseverating on mistakes, miscues, and regret from choices past has no redeeming value and only serves to weigh us down. Not only that, but carrying those burdens needlessly constrains our ability to achieve greatly, or even to function reasonably well, into the future.

There are really only two worthwhile reasons to "look back":

1) To reflect on the work, lives, and legacy of consequential others who preceded us, and
2) To learn from the past.

One of the most predominant toxins preventing us from living well is a refusal to forgive. Let us forgive, ourselves *and* others, and move toward a better future.

Under the Lights

As a high school football coach for 15 years early in my professional career, I found it amazing that thousands of young men show up for two-a-day football practices in the heat each summer. Even more perplexing is the number of those young men that do so knowing full well that the deck is stacked against them. Many of these teams know their prospects of having a great season are not good, and even of having an average season are minimal. Yet, show up they do. Work they do. Sweat, bleed, struggle, they do.

I once posed the question of why all those youngsters undertake such a daunting task, with such high risk of failure, to a large high school faculty. After several awkward moments of pondering, the veteran offensive line coach signaled to me that he thought he knew the answer. His response: "They do it for Friday nights. For the chance to perform under the lights."

Of course they do! Whenever we give team members the chance to somehow display their work in front of an audience, the level of engagement goes up, the level of commitment goes up, and the quality of work goes up. Our game improves when we know others will be watching.

Worthy vision for any organization must somehow include the prospect of "playing under the lights."

Boundaries

Boundaries are viewed in many ways. Here are several of them:

- A demarcation that designates ownership.
- Imaginary borders that represent a difference in context.
- Understood off-limits subjects of conversation.
- Divisions, real or imagined, that separate groups of people.
- Spoken or implied limits to which one's aggressiveness must stop.
- Partitions that "contain" different lines of authority.
- An endpoint or "wall" at which one must stop, literally or figuratively.
- The limit of our mental, physical, or emotional endurance.

The boldest thinkers and the most courageous leaders I know usually view boundaries as opportunities for new breakthroughs, for higher levels of achievement, as horizons of new innovation or creation, as potentialities for new alliances. Very often their dreams and aspirations (i.e., their vision for the organization) simply *begin* at the boundaries. They steadfastly refuse to simply stop at the boundary and shrug as if "that's it."

Hope's Mirage

Any vision we have of a better future is built on hope. Hope, however, is only a mirage, a figment of our imagination. While hope is arguably a necessary motivator for us, it is an abstraction that in and of itself has no power. What really moves us toward our vision is a concrete plan of action, deliberate steps to be taken, firm commitments of time, resources, and effort.

While hope is a beautiful thing, it is really nothing more than wishful thinking. Realizing those aspirations can only occur when we've intentionally committed ourselves to achieving those dreams.

So, absolutely, let's place our hope in a better future. Then, let us craft a plan of action that will move us in that direction, making the mirage a reality.

Forecasting

One of my mentors impressed upon me the power of forecasting.

Forecasting is a pre-flective (as opposed to reflective) process that consists of several steps:

1) Thinking about potential problems and upcoming conversations/decisions,
2) Considering all the possible pathways that those events *might* take, and
3) Considering carefully how we, as leaders, can respond to the natural flow of those potentialities/eventualities.

It's not manipulation; it's not voodoo. It's careful and thoughtful cognition about possibilities and opportunities. Forecasting does not necessarily prevent train wrecks, nor does it ensure fluid progress toward goals and vision. It can, however, assist us in averting problems and influencing positive outcomes.

Forecasting *can* help us react/respond more wisely, with fewer hiccups, and less loss of time/energy/resources (and sometimes even, life or limb).

The underlying assumption, of course, is that we are actually *paying attention* to the things going on around us.

Accelerator or Brake?

I once heard leadership analogized with the act of driving a car. As drivers we make thousands of decisions (most rather unconsciously) about when to press the accelerator and when to press the brake. In fact, there are thousands (if not millions) of shades of gray between those two acts. Knowing how much accelerator or how much brake to apply, and more importantly, when to apply them, is a skill that is learned over time. Yet each new day of driving provides us opportunities and challenges that are similar, yet not quite the same, as the ones we have faced before.

In leadership, as in driving, we are compelled to speed up and slow down on a continual basis, personally, in our relationships, and with respect to the organizations we lead. And, what evidence do we use to make those decisions to speed up or slow down? It is the stimuli — the data, the feedback, the results — we encounter. In driving a car, those stimuli are things such as environmental conditions, the signage and regulations, safety considerations, levels of risk, defensive considerations, desired time of arrival, etc. Very similar kinds of stimuli exist for us in the leadership realm. The underlying assumption is that we are actually paying attention to the stimuli.

Yet, in leadership (just as in driving) the objective is always the same - to get us (and those in the vehicle/organization with us) to a desired destination, safely, within an optimal window of time.

Distracted driving is a huge problem. Distracted leadership is a bigger one. Are we pressing the accelerator or tapping the brake? With how much pressure? How long? And most importantly, why?

Vision and the Sunflower

Ever notice how sunflowers constantly face the sun as it makes its way across the sky? The same holds true, I think, of powerful organizational visions. When a vision has that powerful magnetism which compels attention (like the sun compels the attention of the sunflower) members of the organization are drawn to its allure, all day, every day. They find themselves focusing on it without really having to think about it.

Does the vision for/of your organization, either stated or implied, have that kind of magnetic power for your membership?

6

Ethical Behavior: Rightness, Fairness, Steadfastness

> *"In a real sense all life is interrelated. All men are caught in an inescapable network of mutuality, tied into a single garment of destiny. Whatever affects one directly, affects all indirectly. I can never be what I ought to be until you are what you ought to be, and you can never be what you ought to be until I am what I ought to be. This is the interrelated structure of reality."*

> - MARTIN LUTHER KING, LETTER FROM BIRMINGHAM JAIL

Believing and Caring

When we look back through history at powerful leaders who have had huge and lasting impact on others, we can see a couple of common indicators:

1) Those consequential leaders **believed** uncompromisingly in their cause. Though they may not have understood completely where their leadership would ultimately "take" the tribe (in fact, few leaders know this), they believed strongly in the tenets, the vision, and the rightness of their *direction*.

2) Those powerful leaders **cared** deeply about their followers. The best of our leaders understand that many sacrifices are made along followership's path. None of us have enough time/energy/resources to do everything that is important. Choosing to invest in a particular vision/cause implies choosing *not* to spend our time/energy/resources

on some other ones (even though they may be worthy ones). The best leaders understand the commitment behind those choices and reciprocate with *care*.

Authentic leaders understand that forced compliance is not leadership. When others volunteer to follow a cause/vision, their best efforts follow (without compliance elements like excessive monitoring, sanctions, penalties, score cards, hierarchies, etc.). When folks are coerced or forced into followership, their best efforts rarely ensue.

Here are two important questions for leaders to consider:
How deeply do I believe in the rightness of the direction/vision I'm pursuing?
How much do I care (and show it) for those who choose to follow along?

Subversives

Almost all organizations, no matter how small or how large, have some members who are subversives. These characters generally operate at levels a little more egregious than simply being resistors or recalcitrants. Subversives are the folks who actively and intentionally attempt to undermine and derail processes and/or other people in the organization.

Motivations for subversive behavior vary, but among them are jealousy, fear, ambition, laziness, and disdain. Whatever the motivations, subversives usually rely on organizational secrecy, miscommunication, and privilege as the transmission vehicles of their toxins.

While dealing with subversives is one of the most challenging (and discouraging) tasks of leaders, here are a few simple modes of operation we can use to make the work of subversives more difficult:

- Model and insist upon transparent communications within the organization, both vertically and horizontally. No secrets!

- Have conversations about organizational challenges in open forums, where all members are invited to listen and all members have a voice.
- Confront subversives directly with the evidence of their duplicity, as often as that evidence emerges.

When we keep the work of the organization fully in the light of day, the subversives have a much more difficult time enacting their dastardly deeds.

Pretending

Pretending is something we all do at one time or another.

Sometimes we pretend in order to appear to be someone/thing we're not.
Sometimes we pretend just to get through a difficult time.
Sometimes we pretend in order to fool others.
Sometimes we pretend in order to fool ourselves.
Sometimes we pretend in order to escape from reality (even if briefly).

One way or the other, pretending amounts to suspending our authenticity and misrepresenting the "real" us.

For amusement or entertainment, perhaps pretending is an acceptable diversion. However, if we find ourselves pretending all the time, just to survive, it's time to take a careful assessment of the "why."

Our fullest lives, our optimum health, our maximum happiness, our peak performance flows from being authentically ourselves. It springs from a tight alignment between our aspirations/dreams and our beliefs/enactments.

If we are pretending to be engaged in our work, pretending in our relationships, pretending in our commitments, pretending to be happy, it's time for a reality check. And, a change in behavior.

Accountability Systems

As an observer of accountability systems over many years, here are some common aspects I've seen:

- The more detailed and expansive the accountability measures, the greater the likelihood of failure (often by design).
- Those who seem most endeared to strident accountability standards are usually the ones least likely to be involved in the dirty and difficult work required on the front lines of compliance.
- The creators and proponents of high stakes accountability are typically inclined to exempt themselves from the same sort of expectations, scrutiny, oversight and consequences. The political ruling class fits well in this category.
- Externally imposed accountability never works as efficiently or effectively as that that is locally developed, monitored, and/or enforced.

Accountability is, in concept and deployment, an attempt to impose the wishes of one group/individual upon another group/individual, regarding behavior or performance. And, it is usually most effective when there is means to punish or penalize those who fail to meet the expectations of said others.

The purest and most authentic accountability is intrinsically driven. It's a mindset that is taught, not imposed; modeled, not demanded.

Weed Eaters

Weed eaters are wonderful tools. They're usually powered by gasoline engines or electric current, and give us the ability to cut/eliminate a LOT of weeds in a real big hurry. They are made for destruction and rarely fail to deliver on that front.

The down side is that the weed eater has no ability to discriminate. When powered up it takes down whatever the operator directs it toward. Thus, too often the weed eater also becomes a flower, grass, tree, paint, fence, and/or window eater as well. Not good.

The same sort of good-tool-gone-awry dynamic happens in organizations when we craft procedures and protocols aimed at the "weeds" among us. Maybe the weeds get eliminated, maybe not. Too often, many non-weeds fall victim, as a side effect, to the destructive tools we create.

Damage thereby done is very slow to heal...

Steady at the Helm

Leaders of groups and organizations are much like a helmsman on a ship, the person in charge of steering the ship. The helmsman is supposed to get us to our desired destination, safely, soundly, and on time. Here are some attributes of quality helmsmen:

- They understand the limits of their boat, getting the most out of it without pushing it beyond its capabilities.
- They have thoroughly studied the routes to be taken and steer clear of danger.
- They keep a wary eye on the weather and contextual conditions at all times.
- They know that the success of the journey is dependent on MANY other sailors on the boat, which have skills and expertise they likely do not possess themselves.
- They are focused and clear-headed, always keeping their attention on getting to the goal.
- They are emotionally strong, resilient, and unflappable.
- They learn quickly from the wisdom of others, and from their own mistakes.
- They understand that their cargo is precious and treat it as such.

- They take the shortest, safest route to the destination, and are disinclined to take diversions.
- They know when to speed up and when to slow down, when to steer to port and when to steer to starboard.
- They understand that safety trumps speed and execution trumps strategy.

"Steady at the helm" is more than just an old sailor's axiom, it's a state of being that is greatly desired for those who presume to lead others.

Steady as she goes, mate.

Winning, But Losing

Sometimes you win.................................but you lose.
Sometimes you lose................................but you win.

Those paradoxical admonitions were embedded in my psyche by one of my mentors.

Proving others wrong may be within our capability. Trumping their decisions may be within our authority. Undoing or devaluing their work may be within our power. Making them look or feel foolish may be something within our reach (in fact, we may wish it - with or without justification).

In leading others, there is a price to be paid for "winning" at the expense of others. Like a soap bubble, our "winning" is visible and tangible but for a moment; yet it pops and disappears rather quickly. Like rot, their "losing" grows slowly and consumes *us* over time.

Making ourselves look or feel better, or achieve more, at the expense of others in our organization carries a hefty long-term price, the bill for which will most certainly come due.

Always, Sometimes, or Never

How would your family, your friends, your colleagues, or your customers describe you on a scale of integrity?

Would they say you:

a) ALWAYS do what you say you'll do
b) SOMETIMES do what you say you'll do
c) NEVER do what you say you'll do

Consider the implications of their responses for your happiness (and theirs) and your success (and theirs).

It's also kind of invigorating (or frightening) that we actually have so much control over how they might view us in this regard.

Hide-and-Seek

Hide-and-Seek is a great game. For kids. Not so much for leaders, however. Hiding from problems, dodging tough calls, avoiding accountability is a fool's game that many in leadership try to play. But they'll be found (out), sooner or later.

Servant leaders operate in broad daylight, out in the open. They do so by:

- Being fully transparent.
- Communicating the same message, pervasively, to all stakeholder groups.
- Confronting threats to organizational wellbeing honestly, openly, expeditiously.
- Having high expectations - first for themselves, then for everyone else.
- Taking the risk of giving autonomy to others to "get the job done."

- Minimizing the insulating layers between themselves and the customer, and between themselves and the folks who are "getting the job done."
- Staying centered on values, rather than policies/procedures/protocols.
- Treating the have-nots and the have-it-alls with the same level of respect.

Ethical leadership demands no less.

Shot Taking

In the field of conflict resolution there is a concept known as "unfair fighting." That notion refers to tactics used that tend to turn the conflict into bitter dispute based in nuance, accusation, recrimination, and vagary rather than toward an authentic attempt at resolution. The cheap shots of unfair fighting are often leveraged in order to skirt the real issues, to divert attention, and/or to center the dispute on personal rather than issue-based data. The objective of unfair fighting is to ensure that one party wins and the other loses, truth be damned, peaceful resolution be doomed.

I recently watched a video that was purported to be an academic discussion about the spiritual aspects of our humanity and the implications for our collective future. The discussion panel included representatives of the agnostic, atheist, religious, spiritual, and mystic perspectives. All the participants were highly educated, immensely credentialed, and notably respected within their fields.

While the conversation was intriguing and enlightening, I was disappointed to repeatedly hear the cheap shots so often associated with unfair fighting being taken. Cheap shots, even when subtly couched as compliments, do nothing to contribute to healthy discourse. Moreover, they usually serve to derail informative debate.

Almost without exception, the cheap shots of unfair fighting make the shot taker look and sound weak, uninformed, and defensive. Cheap shots never lead to positive outcomes.

Wise leaders know better, and refrain from using such cheap shots.

Ethical Angels

When we aspire to do worthy and meaningful work, it means investing ourselves fully in the process. And, worthy and meaningful work can rarely be done in isolation. It requires us to work with and to partner with others in that endeavor.

We must choose our partners wisely. Engaging in worthy and meaningful work with a team of ethical angels is one of the most fulfilling of experiences. Such pursuits usually entail a noble mission, fully committed participants, highly functional teamwork, mutual support, respectful and trust-centered interactions between the partners, etc. It feels almost heavenly.

Hitching our wagon, on the other hand, to less-than-ethical angels is a lot like living in.............hell.

Exploitation

We see exploitation occurring everyday. Exploitation is irresponsibly and unfairly using/misusing/abusing other humans or natural resources.

Examples of exploitation include the senseless consumption of natural resources, taking credit for the work of others, hubris in all its forms, abuse in all its forms (physical, mental, emotional, and social), insider trading, and bullying.

So, what is our responsibility as humans? Our existence in this universe calls upon us to fully respect the time, bodies, person-ness, and space of others, and to dance symbiotically with Nature as if our very lives depend on Her (because they do).

We must object overtly to exploitation when we see it. To not do so is to condone it.

Boomerang

Nothing makes us smaller than when we disparage someone else.

Nothing makes us weaker than when we point out the weakness(es) of others.

Nothing makes us more ludicrous than when we make fun of others.

Nothing disgraces us more than when we behave disrespectfully toward others.

Nothing impugns our honor more than when we spread hurtful gossip about others.

Denigration has a built-in boomerang effect. Trying to make others smaller never results in our getting bigger. Trying to make ourselves bigger at the expense of others always makes us smaller.

"Do unto others as you would have them do unto you." - Luke 6:31

Golden. And so simple.

Right's Hubris

If feels just so darned good to be right, huh?

When, after the debate, the comparing of data, the argumentation of "the facts," our declaration of position, it is deeply gratifying to have "won" in the arena of comparative analytics.

Time, then, to break out the champagne, to celebrate our rightness, to take that victory lap, to high-five our alike thinkers.

There's a gnawing problem, however. I can't remember a single time that I've proudly and bombastically proven someone else wrong that has paid long-lasting benefits when it comes to maintaining a healthy relationship with that other.

Please don't misunderstand. It's okay to make a reasoned case, to state our position, to be clear about our beliefs, to joust in the arena of ideas. It's just not helpful (now or in the future) to make other people feel less for not sharing our position.

Principle Centered

We see and abhor it all the time: Some who hold positions of leadership become "lost" (or, they may have never known "the way" in the first place). These leaders (whether parents, bosses, generals, or politicians) seem committed to making decisions with two objectives in mind:

1) Maintain and secure their position of leadership, and
2) Make their personal lives cheesier (no matter the impact on others).

This mindset and behavior is what I think of as *principle-less* leadership.

The leaders I prefer to follow (and admire and support and emulate) operate from a completely different paradigm. They communicate, make decisions, and commit acts consistent with their principles, regardless of trending sentiment, regardless of short-term advantage, regardless of poll data.

Those principles can come in a lot of packages and can be articulated in many ways, but here are just a few worthy examples:

- *WE* are more important than *I* am.
- The least of us is just as important as the greatest of us.
- What we say/do/decide today should provide positive outcomes for future generations.
- Truth must always trump dishonesty.

Each of us gets to choose how we operate our lives on a daily basis. Oddly, principle-centered leadership not only serves others better, but it is far more self-actualizing for the leader himself/herself. Leading from sound principles is very much like the root system of a mighty tree - it secures us, it feeds us, it grounds us, and it bolsters us in the angriest of storms.

Volunteers

Organizational leaders should view and treat employees as volunteers (rather than as servants or subordinates). Why?

- We have to "win" the investment of the volunteers' contributions, which makes us examine deeply our motivations for their desired responses and the actual *need* for those responses. In effect, are our expectations of them worthy, noble, and tightly aligned to our actual goals?
- We naturally tend to treat volunteers from a basis of equity, with attendant respect.
- We freely offer appreciation and gratitude to volunteers (through varied means).
- We understand that we *NEED* the volunteer, thus we go to great lengths to avoid alienating them.
- We work to build strong, positive, and lasting relationships with volunteers, knowing that such relationships serve both their interests and ours over time.
- We approach differences of opinion or contentious situations with volunteers much more gently and empathetically, in the interest of preserving those relationships.
- We often include volunteers in the setting of expectations, establishing norms, and determining metrics of accountability.

Poor Performers

Every organization has its share of poor performers. In fact, most of us are guilty of performing poorly at one point or another. However, poor performance does not necessarily indicate poor character or even poor work ethic. Typically, poor performance springs from one of two fundamental root causes:

1) An imbalance in our mind-body-spirit wholeness, or
2) Misalignment between our strengths and our work requirements.

Some non-root cause triggers of poor performance look like this:

- Sometimes a person just doesn't "fit," their goals don't align even marginally with those of the organization.
- Sometimes folks are carrying some very heavy personal burdens (e.g., poor health, a troubled marriage, an ill child, horrible nutrition, financial difficulties, caring for aging parents, etc.).
- Sometimes organizational members perform poorly because they simply don't know what the goals of the organization are.
- Sometimes members get "stuck," such as when their role has become so routine and stale, causing them to lose enthusiasm.
- Sometimes, due to a lack of authority or demonstrated confidence by leadership, folks feel helpless to act in the interest of customers.
- Sometimes (but rarely) they simply don't care. They are only there to clock in, clock out, and go home.

It's fairly easy to trace each of these issues back to one of those two root causes shown above. And, the list I provided is certainly not exhaustive.

Addressing problems of mind-body-spirit balance is pretty challenging as it requires a commitment to fully attending to one's total wellness, as we considered in Chapter 3. Proper nutrition, exercise, and rest for the body; attention to personal learning and growth for the mind; and the purposeful commitment to a higher way of thinking/living for the spirit.

Research in the field of psychology suggests that we perform best when we are either in a work role that is well aligned to our strengths, or in a work role that can be "morphed" in a way that allows us to take advantage of our strengths. Buckingham and Clifton (2001) developed the Strengths Finder tool to help us gain a clearer and well-defined picture of our strengths (you can explore it here: https://www.gallupstrengthscenter.com/Home/en-US/Index).

So, what's a person to do? From the first-person perspective, working on our own holistic wellness and achieving strengths-roles alignment is difficult, but very doable. From a third-person perspective (i.e., supervisor's/mentor's), we can't force either corrective action on others. Our best course of action is to help educate (and learn with) others, in order for all of us to come to a deeper understanding of what is causing the poor performance in the first place.

Interestingly, from decades of trying to tease high performance out of team members, I can't recall a single person whom I believe set out each morning with the express purpose of performing badly. It's really not in our nature to *want* to underachieve. Thus, the seeds of improvement already lie dormant, awaiting life-generating impetus. That understanding-the-root-cause element is sort of like the germinating conditions for those dormant seeds. We can do this, to improve our own performance. And, we can help others move in a better direction, too.

Leadership's Plural

It is often said that leadership is a lonely business. To be sure, the toughest decisions in an organization find a way of persistently floating up the hierarchical chain until they land on the desk of the leader. As the plaque on United States President Harry S. Truman's desk in the Oval Office stated, "The buck stops here."

For the most part, leaders understand this phenomenon and accept that finality of authority that comes with the turf. However, the best leaders are also keenly aware that leadership is not a job for isolationists. They have learned (or will) that the best sort of leadership is when the folks in each nook and cranny of an organization are enlisted and empowered in the leadership web. These are the leaders that major in empowerment. They invest in the members of the organization in structural ways, in resource allocation, in education and development, in the distribution of authority, and in relationship building. These are the kinds of leaders that understand that leadership is really a plural concept, not singular.

It's the PEOPLE!

Fancy plans, complex systems, robust programs, high-sounding projects are nothing other than stuff. Success can never be built around these things, simply because they are *things*.

Success only comes as result of the effort of *people*. When people, especially teams of people, coalesce around a powerful idea/pursuit, then and only then does the "stuff" mentioned above make a difference.

A leader's time is far better spent on finding, recruiting, co-opting, and developing people than it is spent on all those other things.

You can't lead stuff; you can only lead people.

Best Magnets

My favorite mentors (of which there are many) possess the magical ability of being able to draw out the best of others. How do they do it? They astutely assess the talents others possess and fashion avenues of pursuit that would allow said others (like you and me) to exercise those gifts to the fullest. Those skillful leaders also avoid spending a lot of time, energy, effort, and capital on trying to "fix" others in the areas in which they are not naturally talented. For instance, they would never try to make a post player (in basketball terms) out of a 5' 2" point guard.

A simple formula for getting the best from others might be framed this way:

Notice the gifts others bring to the table
Optimize the opportunities for those gifts to be used
+   Minimize requiring others to function in their non-gifted areas
=   Stronger relationships and higher levels of performance

They

The word "they" is one we often use to hide behind some assumptions, fears, or insecurities. It usually goes like this: *They always... They would never... They don't... They feel... They hate...*

By impersonalizing the other, we give ourselves permission to characterize them in ways that are convenient to us. It is far easier to paint others,

especially those we don't know, in broad strokes, with vivid colors, and clear lines of demarcation.

However, when we think carefully about the people we truly *KNOW* in some of those categories (e.g., conservatives, liberals, Christians, Muslims, hicks, goths, athletes, republicans, democrats, Baptists, Catholics, geeks, gang bangers, etc.), our assumptions about what *THEY* are like often get turned upside down.

What usually happens when I actually take the time to engage with a person I don't know, to listen to them carefully, to interface with them on a personal level, is that I end up realizing what a mistake it is for me to assume things about them. Many things. *ANYTHING* about them based on their politics, their religion, their color, their age, their economic status… *THEY* usually turn out to be far more like me than I assumed, or could have even conceived.

THEY are almost always very similar to me in these kinds of ways:

- Wondering if we're *really* making a difference.
- Not as certain about things as we would like to be.
- Worried about the state of our nation/world.
- A little apprehensive about what old age holds for us.
- Struggling to make ends meet.
- Wanting the very best for our children and grandchildren.
- Praying to stay (or get) healthy.
- Hoping we're at least marginally close in our approach to spirituality.

When I actually get to *KNOW* the other, *THEY* almost always turn out to be a whole lot like me.

Here's to more knowing, and less judging.

7

Communication: The Most Essential Tool of Leadership

"Leadership is communicating to people their worth and potential so clearly that they come to see it in themselves."

- STEPHEN COVEY (2004)

The Most Essential Tool

Being effective as leaders is dependent on a host of variables. Some are outside, but most well within, our locus of control. No element impacts our ability to lead effectively more than our ability to communicate. How our message is received is determined greatly by how it is communicated.

More than any other time in history, we have available to us a plethora of communication tools with which to connect with our audience(s). Those include blogs, podcasts, email, videos, newsletters, Tweets, Instagram posts, direct marketing, Pinterest, paid advertising, Facebook, and microbursts (such as Pandora ads and pop-ups). Each day seems to bring a new way to communicate with our customers, associates, friends, and family.

Through the way we communicate we signal our vision, our beliefs, our values, our transparency, our vulnerability, our passion, even our love. In large part, our communications are a process of demystifying complexity for our organization's members, our clients, and our external publics.

People listen to and watch EVERYTHING leaders do, thus messages are couched in both spoken and unspoken words, in acts of commission as well as omission. They pay attention to words, to posture, to intonation, to every conceivable nuance. There is nothing we can do about this, except be aware of the messages we send through these various delivery mechanisms and be very intentional about those messages.

One of the primary roles of leaders is to emphatically, consistently, and effectively keep members of the organization focused on the primary mission of the organization. In effect, our job is to manage the attention of the organization, keeping it focused on our vision, mission, and goals. The art of effective communication is getting those messages across, in simple, clear, concise, and memorable ways.

At Ease

Two words that have become clear indicators of effective leadership for me are these: Transparency and Vulnerability.

I had the good fortune to get to observe and know an exceptional leader who exhibited both in exemplary fashion (I'll call him Pat). Pat had the most remarkable ability to make people feel comfortable from the very first moments of interacting with him. Pat had the power to put folks "at ease."

After much reflection on how Pat could emanate that kind of presence, it became clear to me that he managed to manifest those two qualities – transparency and vulnerability – through his words, his attire, his demeanor, his posture, his questions, his eye contact, his tone of voice, and his responses. Pat effectively made others feel valued, important, heard, and elevated. No wonder others enjoyed his leadership and prospered under it. No wonder the organization he led performed so well. No wonder the people that worked with Pat were so endeared to him.

Making people feel at ease is critical to their acceptance of us. That is largely done as a product of first impression.

The Stories We Tell

One of the best morsels of advice I have ever received is related to giving speeches. I was told to never give a speech, but rather, to tell compelling stories. Stories capture the imagination and make powerful personal connections. Stories give meaning to abstractions.

In many ways, the role of the leader is to be that of the organization's "narrator." We tell the stories, recall the important history, describe the challenges, and paint the vision. We tell stories about our heroes, the characters who embody our noblest abstractions. Through our stories we build (or influence) the memories of constituents. We keep alive certain hallmark moments or events. And, we clearly communicate the *meaning* of our work, the worthy purpose of our collective efforts.

The folk tales, the rituals, and the history of the organization, conveyed and shaped through story, is a much stronger adhesive than any organizational manual. Wise leaders and storytellers are cognizant of the need to speak from both the rational and the emotional perspectives. They understand that the best stories are not only heard, but also experienced. And, they make sure those stories always have underlying lessons, lessons that guide us to better futures.

Buy What?!?

Sinek (2010) makes a compelling case that the thing that attracts followers – and their subsequent effort, and time, and energy, and resources – is a compelling story with which they can connect at an emotional level. According to Sinek, they follow "not because they have to, but because they *want* to."

People invest themselves in compelling and worthy messages/causes/dreams/endeavors. Not stuff.

Thus, I'm asking myself these questions more and more frequently:

Am I sold on what I'm selling?
Am I being clear about the "why"?

Am I painting a clear picture about our common pursuit?

Is that common pursuit something noble and worthy and attainable?

Am I maintaining a laser-like focus on the "why," not the "what" or the "how"?

Am I providing succinct and understandable words to capture our common vision?

The answers to those questions can give us a clear indication of who might be "buying," and whether or not what we're "selling" is worth the purchase.

What They See

The word "integrity" originates in the Latin, meaning "whole" or "complete." From the same root springs the word "integrate," which implies a melding, a combining, a merging of various components. When we, as individuals, are "integrated" (or "whole"), we manifest the same persona in all aspects of our lives.

Being a person of integrity conveys to others an aura of consistency, of steadiness, of dependability, of what-you-see-is-what-you-get-edness. That consistency is manifested by a very tight and intentional alignment (or melding) of our beliefs, our words, our actions, our attitudes, our performance(s), our commitments with our values.

"What happens in Vegas stays in Vegas" has an amusing ring to it, and the marketers that use that line most likely generate a lot of money on behalf of Las Vegas. The essence of that message, however, is one that suggests that it is okay to be a different person in different contexts. It indicates a degree of disingenuousness. And, it implies that inconsistency is acceptable.

IF we decide to be persons of integrity, then some hard choices follow about *who/what* we want to be. It means bringing into alignment our three-dimensional selves (emotional/spiritual, intellectual, and physical) in a disciplined way. It means pursuing the eventuality that what others see in us *really is* what they get.

Defining Ourselves

It's a lot easier to define ourselves, and our organizations, by describing the things we're not (or don't want to be). It's much harder to be crystal clear about what we want to be, where we want to go, why we want to go there, and how we plan to get there.

I once saw a news byte on a local television station about a hotly debated issue in our community. The television journalist decided to do one of those man-on-the-street interviews to gauge public sentiment on the issue. The reporter approached an older gentleman who was wearing a John Deere cap, flannel shirt, and denim overalls. The reporter started the conversation by saying something like, "Sir, we're doing a survey to see how folks feel about…" Before she could finish the sentence the old man said, "Yeah, I'm agin' it!"

Interesting to me was the fact that he didn't really seem to care what the topic/issue was, he just knew he was "agin' it." Clearly, he had no clear conception of, nor interest in, the public policy issue at hand, especially if it meant some kind of change in the current status. The community leadership, which was promoting movement toward a better future, had certainly not made a compelling case for their initiative (for this gentleman, at least).

Every organization, every community, every team has the I'm-agin'-it group. Sometimes they can be convinced of need for improvement, sometimes not. They will **never** be convinced if a clear and believable better future hasn't been articulated and defined. The way we define ourselves is critical in gaining support for continuous improvement efforts.

Defining ourselves, personally and organizationally in positive ways, aligned with noble intentions, with clear and doable action steps (even if baby steps), is a prerequisite to meaningful movement toward betterness (yep, another invented word).

Far better than taking a this-is-not-me/us approach is to:

1) Have a clear idea of who/what we want to be,
2) To commit to pursuing those goals relentlessly, and
3) Saying so publicly, often and in a positive way.

Somebody has to make that case, and leaders are the best positioned to do so.

Information Conduits

Information flows, whether we want it to or not. Always has, always will. Even the most oppressive and restrictive governments on Earth now know, without question, that they cannot control the flow of information.

Information can run through a myriad of conduits: carrier pigeons, ambassadors, smoke signals, Pony Express riders, telegraph, lanterned night-riders, phones, television, advance scouts, telepathy, social media, etc. The list goes on without end. In today's environment that information flows almost instantly, and it gets ricocheted through other portals endlessly.

While we can't control what others say/think about us, we can control what we communicate about ourselves. The only question is what message(s) do we want to send? We have the power to frame the opinions and impressions of others, but we must be intentional in the process.

What signals are we sending? Are they the ones we want sent?

Symbols and Rituals

The physical symbols we display reinforce our values and beliefs. The rituals we choose to practice serve as the validation and the perpetuation of many of our stories. Our values tend to diminish or become diluted over time unless they are deliberately codified, regenerated, and embedded (in ways both overt and covert) into the collective psyche of the organization. Symbols and rituals play an important role in this process.

Most organizations and most leaders find ways to recognize and incentivize achievement. Too few, however, understand the even more powerful effects of praising effort. Learning how to affirm others authentically and freely for their effort in pursuing the collective vision is critical. Sutton (2010) points out that *EVERYONE* wins when the leader gives as much credit as possible to others and takes as little credit as possible for him/herself. Expressing appreciation and affirmation is a learnable art, and it's extremely powerful from a symbolic perspective. Leaders should always affirm, always thank, always acknowledge, and always give others credit. Deliberately choosing symbols and enacting rituals to those ends pay immeasurable dividends.

Forums, Not Boxes

Organizations for decades have used the concept of suggestion boxes to solicit ideas for improvement. More often than not they become the vehicle for negativism. Complaints, cheap shots, snide remarks abound – all anonymously delivered. I'm not a fan of suggestion boxes. However, I am a fan of garnering as much feedback as one can in order to make the wisest decisions possible on behalf of an organization.

A far better approach to soliciting feedback/perspective is to have forums or small group meetings in which leaders actually *engage* the members of the organization in dialogue about ideas for improvement, areas which need attention, processes/policies that aren't working. When substantive dialogue occurs among/between organizational members from all levels, worthy ideas percolate to the top. Perspectives are gained. Voices are heard. Opinions are shared. Troubleshooting occurs. Possibilities are teased out.

Not everyone likes that kind of process, however. Those who refuse to participate in those dialogues are often the ones who know their thoughts will not withstand the scrutiny of open discourse. They are the ones, incidentally, who much prefer the suggestion box.

Watched

I heard it for years – from my parents, from my grandparents, from my teachers, from my coaches, from my principals, from my preachers, and from my bosses. What did I hear? "You are being watched. *All* the time." Mostly the watchers are friends, loved ones, and impressionable children. But not always. Our enemies and those who wish us ill watch us, too.

As I became a husband, a father, a grandfather, a teacher, a coach, a mentor, a principal, a superintendent, a boss, I found myself often and forever reminding the folks within my sphere of influence that they were being watched, too. Mostly by their friends, loved ones, adoring students. But not always. Their enemies and those who wish them ill watch, too.

Since our actions really do speak FAR louder than our words ever do (or will), it is well worth the effort to spend a little time reflecting on what all those others are seeing when they watch us.

Beware the Closed Door

Those who work with and around me know that I rarely close my office door, even if I'm having a meeting with someone. I believe transparency rules (or should). Generally, organizational issues are best dealt with from a full-and-open-disclosure mindset, and similarly aligned environment. Any business conducted behind closed doors automatically arouses suspicion, which usually fosters lack of trust. Trust is the golden commodity.

Supply problems, profit-loss concerns, organizational morale issues, technology hiccups, etc., belong to the organization and efforts to hide or conceal those from its members are acts of futility (if not outright insanity). Secrecy often implies conspiracy. Conspiracy often implies illegality or unethical behavior. Illegality or lack of ethics cost us respect, business, profit, and TRUST!

Ronald Reagan is said to have famously noted that "the walls have ears." Indeed. We should think twice about closing the office door (I think it best to do so only when personal privacy issues are the primary concern).

Trust is a "force multiplier" (a phrase I learned from General Colin Powell, 1995). Anything that causes lack of trust (like lots of closed-door meetings) works to the opposite effect.

The Language We Use

As leaders, the language we use matters, a lot. Communicating in professional language is needful, but communicating in ambiguous, unclear, and evasive language does little else than to make others suspicious of our motives and wary of our intentions. The language we choose can influence others, or it can put them off. The language we use can draw others to us, or it can cause them to seek separation from us. The language we use can clarify our aspirations and intentions for a better future, or it can muddy the water and create inertia.

Wise leaders understand the power of words. They seek precision in the language they use. And, they understand the power of succinctness, that when it comes to effective leadership, less really is more.

Finally, astute leaders also understand that EVERYONE should be communicated with as if they are our boss, our customer, our founder, our underwriter, our stockholder, our employee. When it comes to the language we use, there should really be no difference.

"But, ..."

If you want to stop a conversation dead in its tracks, use the word "but." Rather, consider using the word "and" in place of "but" when involved in substantive dialogues. Using "and" instead of "but" tends to keep the discourse open rather than inhibiting (or prohibiting) the expression of an idea or position by another person.

Another strategy for limiting the use of the word "but" is to pause briefly after another has expressed their thinking/position/idea, then offer a question for consideration. Instead of the conversation stopping effect of using the word "but," the question generates an extension of the dialogue and a freer exchange of ideas. Carefully crafted questions allow the subtle introduction of counter-perspective as a possibility for discussion, rather than a direct rebuttal to the other person's idea/thought.

No To Yes/No

Engaging team members in meaningful and consequential dialogue is almost always triggered by powerful questions. Not just any question will do. Some questions hem up the other person(s) into pre-defined answers. Yes/No questions are a classic example of such thought-stopping responses. Here are some examples:

- Are you pleased with the way our enrollment procedures are working?
- Have you been using your talent to the fullest in your job assignment?
- Do you think we're on the right track with our organizational goals?

These questions call for a simple YES or NO answer, and do little to generate deep thought and rich conversation. They allow folks to pick a response then "retreat." Far better to ask questions that draw the team into substantive discussion.

Questions like:

- What are our highest aspirations for the future of our organization?
- How might we improve our service to customers?
- In what ways are you able to use your talents in this job assignment?

These questions invite us to think about possibilities and betterness, and they induce us to share our thinking publicly. From this sort of dialogue ideas begin to surface and solutions get refined. Thoughtful inquiry, prompted by high quality questions, is the leading edge of continuous improvement.

Abstractions

When we use labels to identify people, such as "Texans," "Russians," "Coulters," "Hispanics," "Cheerleaders," or "Cops," we automatically generalize the individuals who make up the group. Those generalizing terms tend to erase (in our minds) the uniqueness of individuals, depersonalizing them and boxing them into categories. Those categories come with a long list of assumptions that often DO NOT fit the individuals.

For instance, I know some "Christians" who don't manifest or even profess the tenets of the Christian faith. There is no one "Hispanic" culture; there are hundreds of them. All "Texans" do not carry guns. Many "country folks" are the furthest thing from being bumpkins (in case you didn't notice, I just used two generalizations in the same sentence).

With some difficulty we can learn to think and speak of people as individuals rather than as abstractions. It's a challenging learning journey (the last sentence in the paragraph above is case in point). Educational experiences, exposure to media, and the predominant political rhetoric all predispose us to thinking of individuals as representations of broader categories, which are nothing more than abstractions. And often, if not always, those abstractions are the furthest thing from the truth.

People are *NOT* abstractions. Thomas Sowell (2013) counsels that when we talk about, or think about, others in terms of the group labels to which we assign them, we have in effect *erased* them as individuals. Moving away from thinking of and treating people as abstractions will make us much better people and more effective servant-leaders.

Power Words

"I'm sorry." "I goofed." "I messed that up, didn't I?" "My bad." "My mistake."

One of the hardest things for us to do is to admit and own mistakes. It's also one of the most powerful. Realizing and owning our mistakes are critical components in our learning, and are powerful tools in our leadership arsenal. It was and is true of our learning to ride a bike, our learning to dress ourselves, our learning to hit a golf ball, our learning to manage relationships, and our learning to contribute to a team.

Trying to hide mistakes doesn't work well (and it makes us appear weaker).

Trying to blame our mistakes on others doesn't work well (and it makes us appear weaker).

Trying to make our mistakes not look like mistakes doesn't work well (and it makes us appear weaker).

Learning is a function of mistake making. Mistakes are a function of learning.

I or We

Three "wedge" words that alienate, isolate, imply hierarchy, and separate: **I, ME,** and **MINE.**

Three "magnet" words that invite, incorporate, imply equity, and resonate: **WE, US,** and **OUR.**

It's not too hard to see which triad garners love, trust, volunteerism, and enthusiasm for a mission to be accomplished. As leaders, we must train ourselves always to speak *with* others, not *at* them. We can start altering the words that come out of our mouths beginning right now (depending on our objectives, of course).

Yeah, But

IF collaboration,

the introduction of fresh thinking,

inviting/hearing the voice of all stakeholders,

having rich dialogue around complex problems,

the development of strong and positive relationships, and

creating an environment of transparency and full disclosure

are important to the success (even the SURVIVAL) of our community/organization/family, then there are two words that can pretty much assure that we can't and won't succeed (or survive):

"Yeah, but..."

Those words will pretty much have a bulldozing effect on the environmental dynamics listed above (Block, 2002). The speed/power of the adulteration is directly proportional to the rank of the person using the words.

Respect(fulness)

As a youngster I was blessed to have spent a fair amount of time with my grandfather. Though he was no angel (nor did he claim to be), he purposefully ingrained in me a number of powerful beliefs that have shaped me as a person over the years.

One of the powerful lessons Granddad taught me was the difference between *respect* and *respectfulness*. He was a water well driller and windmill man. Thus, he (and for a number of years during my adolescence when I worked for him, we) helped other folks get water from the ground. He/We served folks who were wealthy as well as those who were dirt poor. We worked both for the honorable, and the scoundrel. We worked for those of all skin colors, all beliefs, from all stations in life. Some were very worthy of our respect; others, not so much.

Through our interactions with that vast array of customers, Granddad coached me to understand that respect is something a person earns. Always, and almost intuitively, we understand who deserves our respect, and who doesn't. We often see those who want our respect, perhaps even demand it, go to great lengths to justify it in our (and their own) minds. It simply doesn't work. Respect is something that must be earned, mostly through actions, rarely through words.

On the other hand, Granddad helped me understand the power of treating others respectfully, whether they deserved it or not. We never "win" by treating others disrespectfully, and we almost always raise our standing in the eyes of others when we choose respectfulness as the default of our interactions. Respectfulness is something we can and should afford all others in our interactions with them (even if they have yet to earn our respect). Exhibiting respectfulness preserves the dignity of the other, and is the surest way to enhance the opportunity for a relationship thereafter.

Our **respect** for others tells the world a great deal about the *other* person. Our **respectfulness** toward others tells the world a great deal about *us*.

Affirmation's Juice

Whenever we choose to honor, praise, or magnify positively the work or value of others, we make them *and* ourselves look BIGGER.

Whenever we choose to diminish, dishonor, criticize, or rebuke the work or value of others, the opposite occurs – we make them *and* us look smaller.

With so much to be gained from the former, and so much to lose from the latter, why is there any question about which is the better path to take?

Affirmation almost always "juices" the receiver as well as the sender. It's like using steroids with no side effects. For an added bonus, it's free! It doesn't cost a thing to affirm another person.

However, *noticing* comes first. That requires paying attention, tuning in, being aware. Speaking of noticing, did you notice that the operative verb in the first sentence above is the word "choose"? Yep, it's a choice.

Inflection

In communications there is a convention called "inflection" which is the result of our stressing a particular syllable in a word, altering the cadence or rhythm of our speech, raising or lowering the pitch of our voice, or emphasizing certain words or phrases. Inflection is a nuanced technique designed to gain or refocus attention to the intended and/or underlying meaning of our words.

Leaders have another dimension of inflection that can be leveraged. The way we direct our attention (or not), the things we choose to emphasize (or not), the behaviors we incentivize (or not), and the folks we empower (or not) send powerful signals to others.

Just as we can use words or the sound of our voice to communicate meaning, we also have the power to use a non-verbal form of inflection to communicate meaning. Those overt and sometimes subtle acts serve also to gain or refocus attention to the intended and underlying meaning of our actions/attention/behaviors.

Here's another dimension of inflection. In mathematics, an inflection point is that point on a continuous curve that represents a change of direction. It is, in effect, the point at which "the turning" occurs. We can use both verbal and non-verbal inflection to generate points of inflection, both in the behavior of individuals and in the behavior of the organization. For leaders, some powerful possibilities exist here.

The frequently deployed alternative, of course, is to muddle along, sending unintentional and mushy signals, in thoughtless ways. Since this approach requires the least thinking and work, it makes sense that it is the default setting for so many leaders.

However, for those who aspire for *more*... (Yes, that was an example of inflection.)

Pablum

By definition, "pablum" is bland intellectual fare, insipid writing or speech, trite conceptualizations, or bogus and hollow acts or articulations. One of my colleagues and I have had numerous interesting discussions about the need for succinctness and precision in communications. The more I work with words as a communications tool, the more suspicious I become of lengthy blatherings, put in legalistic terms, couched in myriad qualifiers, always preceded by disclaimers.

Using inconsequential words, tasks, and/or stuff to either obscure or inhibit progress toward clearly defined goals is a common malady in organizations. Sometimes it is manifested through acts of omission, sometimes via acts of commission. Either way, they're not productive and often prohibitive (sometimes, downright destructive).

STOP THE PABLUM!

Listening

Listening is, perhaps, the most powerful item we possess in our toolbox of communications media (Brady, 2003). To learn to listen fully and with complete presence provides for us the opportunity to truly discern not only the message(s) being delivered by others, but also the motivations, interests, and positions that underlie those messages. If we can learn to listen from the heart, with a genuine sense of empathy, we stand an even better chance of fully understanding the "other." In effect, dynamic listening helps us to understand the *essence* of another person.

Oddly, active listening is the one of the least frequently and least effectively practiced communication tools. Being an effective listener tends to "intensify" what we hear. Furthermore, it has the impact of improving what we conse-quently say. Our attention to others is a gift, a most precious gift. Nothing signals that attention like focused listening.

Some things that active listening conveys:

Valuing   *Interest*
               Attention
        Respect   *Concern*   *Calmness*
           Openness   *Acceptance*
   Deliberation   *Curiousness*   *Humbleness*
                   Steadfastness

Hmmm…. I don't see a single word in that group that I wouldn't want folks to think of when they think of me.

What would it be like if others thought of us in those terms? What would it be like if we could think of ourselves in those terms? What would our homes and places of work be like if we could ***listen*** our way through each day in those terms?

No costly training required. We can start right now.

Better Questions

I am convinced that if we learn to ask better questions, we will become better listeners. Moreover, if we become better listeners we stand a better chance to learn more, to understand more fully, and to assess more wisely. Questions are far more powerful and transformational than answers.

Using starter stems like "How would…" and "How can…" and "What might we…" and "Is there a way to…" are much better than "Should…" and "What is…" and "When will…" In short, questions that open doors to broader dia-logue from a wider range of possible participants enrich the dialogue. Question stems that force folks to take a position or provide a concrete "solution" right off the bat tend to narrow the discourse and polarize responses.

Asking the right, and the right kinds of, questions can trigger consequential conversations. Questions that invite and encourage first-person responses are best. Keeping conversations in the first person make them less likely to drift into pontifications in which speakers report on behalf of others (most of whom are not and never will be "in the room"). The very best questions, I find, are those that either directly or indirectly cause folks to compare and contrast two phenomena. This line of inquiry cuts to the very heart of what we know is the way the brain naturally and playfully works as it encounters new or novel stimuli.

"Listen a hole in 'em." In other words, pose questions that invite folks to deeper levels of reflection and thinking. THEN, focus intently on their words, their facial expressions, their body language, their tone, their attention, etc. In effect, we should listen with all our senses, seeking to understand the other as fully as possible. It is not about debate, it's about learning what the other thinks, believes, wants, and needs.

Let silence play its role. As leaders, we must learn to be okay with long moments without words, in which thoughts can be formulated and considered, in which articulations can be considered fully before new words fill the air (and our brains). Far more frequent is the wish that one would have remained silent, than the wish that one would have spoken up.

We can convey openness and interest through the questions we ask and through our responses to the answers given. This is both respectful and inclusive in nature.

Listening's Antecedents
Three prompts can assist us in being more attentive listeners. Here are those three conditioners:

1) Curiosity – We should try to go into each conversation/encounter with a curious mind, in search of hearing/seeing/feeling/learning something we didn't know previously. Engaging with curiosity also helps us ask better questions.
2) Suspend assumptions – We should try to put any presuppositions or assumptions we have about a situation or a person "on the shelf" in order to minimize our biases while hearing the other person out.
3) "What if I'm wrong?" – We should try to go into each conversation with the understanding that we may be proven wrong, or misinformed, or un-enlightened. Adopting an I-may-be-

proven-wrong mindset helps us be more transparent in the discourse, and it helps us accept more freely the perspective of others.

Last-Heard-Itis

I have observed a number of organizational leaders over the years who were guilty of reacting, and making decisions, in response to the last person heard. It is a painful situation to feel like you know what you're supposed to be doing, you understand the direction of the organization, you have a good feel for how things need to be done, you're making organizational progress at a brisk clip, only to have a curve ball thrown at you as a result of someone getting in the ear of a boss who succumbs to "the last person heard."

Every organization I've worked in had a few of those folks who refrained from making their positions known publicly or from engaging in the dialogue/debate, but who always seemed to seek the boss out in private to try to influence (or reverse) decisions. A very common ploy of said characters is that they portend to be speaking on behalf of a whole group of others.

Don't get me wrong. Leaders should *always* listen. But, leaders should be very wary of folks who operate in such clandestine fashion. Arguments or positions, if worthy, should be able to stand the rigor of open discourse. If they can't, the boss shouldn't be giving them credence (even if they do come from "the last person heard").

The Message of Processes

Just as with our words, leaders send powerful messages through the systems and processes we deploy. Every organization has its protocols and processes. Some convey autonomy and ownership to the members of the organization. Some, on the other hand, signal that employees can't be trusted, or are not smart enough, or don't have the authority to do what they think is best. In effect, some leaders, via the processes they craft and/or condone, enslave the organization to those processes. Such organizations are rightly and often vilified as "bureaucratic." There are good reasons for the negative connotations associated with that word.

Skillful attention to the structure and rationale for adopted processes can send powerful and positive signals throughout an organization. Processes such as feedback loops, evaluation systems, induction protocols, even parking arrangements send messages to both internal and external stakeholders.

Yes!

The words of leaders have powerful impact. For example...

"Yes" is a word that triggers the following kinds of responses:

    -Action
      Energy
          -Impetus
              Beginnings
                  -Initiation
              -Enthusiasm
          -Exertion
      -Synergy
    -Effort

"No," on the other hand, generates the following kinds of reactions:

-Disappointment
-Disenchantment
-Acquiescence
-Withholding
-Exhaustion
-Stagnation
-Deflation
-Stopping
-Ending

As leaders of teams and organizations, which list of descriptions embodies the highest prospects?

One of the fundamental tenets of improvisational comedy is to never block the pitch from another comedian with some form of "no." It brings the whole show to a screeching halt. While I would never suggest that leadership behavior should mimic the flow of improvisational comedy (come to think of it, perhaps the proposition is worthy of consideration), it is not lost on me that one of the most creative, interesting, innovative, and entertaining human crafts relies so heavily on "YES".

As leaders, it behooves us to look for more ways to say "YES" and fewer ways to say "NO."

Persnickety
We all know people who major in the minors. They critique, dissect, cajole, nitpick anything and everything. We also know those people as persistent pains and energy drains. It's even worse when they're in charge.

None of us want to be known as one of those persnickety types (not even those who *are* the persnickety types want to be known as such).

So, when is the right time for fastidiousness? We should notice, acknowledge, and address issues under the following circumstances:

- When mistakes become persistent trends.
- When we clearly have folks in the wrong roles.
- When the heartburn is being caused by ethical deficits.
- When a team member is unable or unwilling to get better.
- When those who are responsible are ducking the responsibility.
- When the variance in performance impacts our reputation and/or the quality of products and services.

We should be persnickety only when it really counts (and leave the small stuff alone). If we're persnickety about everything and everybody, we're in for a long and lonely life.

Secrets

I noted earlier that Ronald Reagan is quoted as saying, "The walls have ears." In our organizational lives (regardless of the size of the group), keeping secrets with one set of members and from another set of organizational members is a temptation that must be avoided.

What are some reasons organizations (and people) try to keep secrets? To hide damaging information, to maintain hierarchical privilege, to mask inequitable decisions, to protect perceived advantage, out of fear of dissent and debate, or to protect turf.

What damage is done when organizations (and people) try to keep secrets? Trust is lost, it drains precious human/organizational energy, it distracts from the primary mission(s), it causes inertia among the troops, it creates uncertainty in decision making, it promotes risk aversion, it inculcates isolationism, and it incubates fear.

When you look at those two lists (which are not exhaustive, by any means), it's hard to come to the conclusion that secret keeping serves a useful purpose.

If trust, teamwork, productivity, and full investment are the elements of our aspired culture, then no secrets should be allowed.

When we act and interact from that mindset, then a culture of transparency, full disclosure, and open communications begins to emerge and sustain. Trust is the healthy by-product of such an environment.

It is critical that leaders are saying, signaling, and perpetuating the same information/messages throughout the organizational structures - vertically, horizontally, and obliquely. Thus, every member hears the same thing, in the same way, many times over.

Attempts at secret keeping are very much like metastasizing cancers. They quickly gobble up the health, then life, of the organization.

Wise leaders know that the best operational paradigm to work from is one that presumes that *There Are No Secrets*. (The walls really do have ears.)

Influence Multipliers

Colin Powell (1995), former Chairman of the U.S. Joint Chiefs of Staff and former U.S. Secretary of State, refers to what he calls "force multipliers." These are strategies we can use that accelerate or intensify the impact of an action/campaign/initiative. Think of them as steroids for impact.

According to David Rock (2008) there are certain similar factors (which he calls SCARF) that allow us to magnify our ability to influence others. By reducing the sensation of threat and at the same time leveraging the nuanced impression of reward we can enhance our influence via five domains:

Status - making others feel more important.
Certainty - removing as much uncertainty about the future as possible.
Autonomy - giving others as much control of their own work/destiny as possible.

Relatedness - fostering a sense of safety.

Fairness - cultivating an environment of equity and fair exchange.

Using this SCARF model, we make it easier for others to trust us. It's the "juice" for influence. Or, to channel General Powell, influence multipliers.

Bridges or Walls

Leaders are constantly engaging with others. Some of those others we know, some we don't. With each encounter one of two things occurs, we either build a bridge between us and the other person, or we build a wall.

We make this choice, whether we realize it or not. That bridge or wall we construct is built through our words, our facial expressions, our level of attentiveness, our degree of listening, our disposition, our emotional state, and our body language.

To be happy, successful, and productive in life, we need to build a *LOT* more bridges than walls. In fact, walls are rarely beneficial.

Heartless

Leading requires heart. There are those who think they can lead without it, that they can insulate themselves from caring while leading others. But, any evidence of effectiveness in this regard is chimeral.

Trying to express care through memos or public address announcements doesn't really work. We have to show up, in person. How we can manifest caring? We can notice others, what they're doing, how they contribute, when they hurt. We can help, by lending a hand, by offering support, by rolling up our sleeves and contributing. We can defend the good work and noble effort of those around us who are diligently pursuing our collective goals. We can remember names, past efforts, former campaigns together, and the interests of others. We can touch – through handshakes, hugs, and fist bumps (but don't get weird). We can listen, listen a hole right through 'em. Always listen, too much.

Caring takes work, but the dividends are plentiful. Being heartless, on the other hand, is just another way to dodge our own responsibilities as leaders.

Praise

Praise is the act of expressing appreciation or admiration to/for someone. Praise can be an uplifting, almost worshipful expression, emanating from the very core of our being. Done in that spirit, praise is buoyant for both the praiser and the praisee.

Praise can also be bogus and hollow, expressed with little or no conviction. That kind of praise is icky and diluted. It kind of makes you feel like you need to take a shower after hearing it.

The best leaders I know are masterful in the art of giving authentic praise. They *find* things to praise others for, often and in many ways. These leaders even manage to praise others vicariously, through their colleagues, employees, and family, finding an indirect and sometimes obscure pathway for the praise. Consistently, these leaders praise others in the context of their shared values, beliefs, missions, and vision. The best form of praise is always specific and meaningful.

One of the main reasons these leaders are so *good* is that they actually pay enough attention to the people around them to see/hear/know what is being done by those others that is actually praiseworthy. For that, they deserve our praise.

Barbed Praise

One of the techniques of supervision is to soften the blow of critical feedback by sandwiching it between elements of praise. Most of us have probably been victims of such disingenuous connivery. As soon as the first lines of positive feedback come our way we begin to feel the tension, to expect the barb, to steel ourselves against the expected negative critique (often called "constructive criticism"). The defense shields go up.

To complete the loop, the person offering the negative feedback (often the boss) then tries to soothe the pain by applying the balm of more positive feedback.

Most of us also remember only the negative ("constructive") criticism that came to us through the exchange.

Since none of us accept negative criticism all that well (a fact grounded in research), why not simply offer lots of positive feedback to others? Leaders that offer feedback that is real, legitimate, authentic, and springs from our actually noticing the good stuff they've done, stand to benefit a great deal from such a strategy. Leaders would do well to skip the negative critiques unless/until we're asked for "constructive criticism." When it is requested, deliver it gently and in the form of opening a dialogue about how *we* get better, on purpose, everyday.

Speechless

When we hear someone use the word "speechless" we generally infer exasperation or astonishment at some absurdity. However, "speechless" can be a really good thing for those in leadership positions.

When we **observe** without judgmental or corrective commentary, when we **ask** with intent to learn, when we **listen** without rebutting, and when we **seek** feedback and safely, quietly allow it, we have practiced a very enriching form of speechlessness. Less talking and more authentic *connecting* from leaders is both an energizing and affirming practice. It also happens to pay immeasurable dividends for all parties involved.

Pleasant Score

Pleasant is *way* underrated! It's one of those things most of us intuitively understand, though we rarely think about it. We know those members of our families, our churches, our service clubs, and our workplaces who are consistently pleasant. They're the ones we really like to be around, the ones who make us feel better for having been in their presence, the ones who make the environment they're in richer by just being there. We also know which ones *don't* make us feel that way; they're the ones we dread and avoid if at all possible.

There's not a pleasantness score or scale or barometer or measurement tool (that I know of), but who needs one. Like beauty, we know it when we see it (even though we have a darned difficult time trying to define/measure it). Being pleasant requires no special skills, no degrees, no credentials, no titles. Any of us can be pleasant. Any of us can make being pleasant a habit. There is no cost involved. It's simply a choice.

Default to Polite

There was a bit of tension in the air. My wife and I were clearly not on the same page. That has occurred several times (hundreds?) since we started hanging out with each other over four decades ago. We got past that tense part, as we usually do, and managed to agree on a path forward (sometimes we just agree to disagree, but still move forward).

The way all of us manage conflict has a lot to do with our "default setting," our auto response mode. Conflict happens to all of us (well, maybe not to hermits). When we deal with people, we will most assuredly deal with conflict. When dealing with conflict, people have natural default settings. Some default to anger. Some default to blaming. Some default to argument. Some default to silence. Some default to recrimination. Some default to violence. Some default to acquiescence. Some default to harsh words. Some default to victimhood. Some default to politeness.

Probably no surprise here, but it's much easier to get past the bumpy spots when we default to polite. It allows a little oxygen to return to the room, it mitigates the use of hurtful words, and it enhances the chances of finding some common ground. Defaulting to polite is a learnable skill. And, it's a choice.

Observant

Observing is one of the most powerful tools we have at our disposal. It amounts to focusing, paying attention, being aware, noticing. In being fully observant we have multiple tools available to us by which to take "readings": seeing, listening, sensing, asking, engaging, and/or feeling. Through those processes we can fully participate in our work, and in *LIFE*.

Two big inhibitors that get in the way of our observing are:

1) Going too fast (gotta get stuff done!), and
2) Talking too much.

Every one of the things in both lists above is completely within our control.

Questions?

It happens frequently in my service as a mentor. A mentee will seek my help in dealing with a sticky situation, hoping that I may have a quick solution or a magic elixir. As much as I would love to play the role of Merlin, I simply haven't developed those skills.

But, my advice (and my modeling) to these help-seekers always starts with me asking questions. And, I ask those questions from a truly curious perspective.

Good questions help us to begin to find a way forward, and to develop a better understanding of the root causes of the problems.

Here are some helpful *dos* of asking questions:

- Start with question stems like "What..." and "How..."
- Be fully present and attentive when asking. Ask, look, pause, listen.
- Use words/phrases they use in your next questions.
- Counter feelings of anger/aggression with curiosity and openness.
- Nest all questions in a mindset of continuous improvement.

- Always thank others for helping you get a better grasp of the issue through their time, their input, and their thinking (whether you like what you heard from them or not).

As well, there are some cautionary *don'ts* of asking questions:

- Don't interrogate; gently inquire.
- Don't use "Why..." as the question stem. (It sounds and feels judgmental.)
- Don't immediately jump to conclusions, start issuing directives, or make up new rules.
- Avoid divining solutions until you've asked several questions of several people.

There are some benefits to asking substantive questions:

- The better questioner you become, the better listener you'll become.
- Relational capital is directly proportional to curiosity expressed.
- Problems tend to house their own solutions, but only when we reflectively and collaboratively begin to dissect them. Questions are the lab tools of dissection.
- Others feel more valued when genuinely asked for feedback, input, perspective, ideas, and thinking.
- Getting smarter is a byproduct of asking good questions.

Some sample questions:

- What do I need to know before tackling this problem?
- Who else should I talk to that can help me gain deeper insight into this issue?
- How might we proceed without creating additional burdens on others?
- What might I hear from Bob/Betty when I ask about this?
- What should I be asking that I haven't yet?
- What questions do you have for me?

Every Word

Every word we speak builds up or tears down, enhances trust or compromises it, accelerates improvement or slows it, nurtures relationships or diminishes them, facilitates progress or impedes it, fosters peace or suppresses it.

What we say *matters*. A lot. And, every word we speak influences the words others speak. A lot of powerful, magnifying possibilities exist in those realities.

Noticing

When we get really busy "doing stuff," we often fail to notice. Most of what we fail to notice is in the psyche, the mood, or the emotion of others within our sphere of influence.

Most of us realize that we are highly dependent on those others to help us accomplish our goals, to live happily and harmoniously, to be effective, and to be productive. As leaders, the folks who work with and around us need for us to notice. Notice things like: their pain, their struggles, their troubled relationships, their unfulfilled dreams, their successes, their difficult circumstances, their talents, their wayward children, their financial hardships, etc.

They don't need for us to diagnose or to give advice or to "fix" or to prescribe. They simply need for us to notice. Our noticing is the first step in authentic connectivity between them and us. Once we notice, new channels of communication open up.

Noticing is not about manipulation. It is not about optimizing performance. It's about connecting authentically, deeply, and caringly.

When we incline ourselves to noticing, the noticing gets returned. We are all affirmed and supported when that happens. We really need for others to notice back. In case you hadn't noticed.

8

The Blindspots

"There are none so blind as those that will not see."

- JOHN HEYWOOD (1546)

Blind Spots

When learning to drive we were taught about the "blind spot" just over and behind our left shoulder. It is in this blind spot that other vehicles can be traveling without our knowing it, potentially threatening our safety and wellbeing.

We have similar "blind spots" in our work and personal lives. These not-so-obvious threats to our success, safety, and wellbeing exist just outside our easy view. They represent potential "wrecks" in our performance and effectiveness, all of which can be avoided with some due diligence on our part.

How can we check for those blind spots in our lives?

1) Just as most of us have developed the driving habit of glancing quickly and frequently back over the left shoulder, we can train ourselves through habit to regularly pause and reflect on what we're doing, why we're doing it, and how we might do it better.

2) Rely on trusted others (think of them as our "auxiliary mirrors") to provide us with feedback on what they see us doing, why it appears we're doing it, and how we might do it better.

Checking our personal blind spots really amounts to practicing a continuous improvement version of "double vision" - regularly taking a look at ourselves in a 360 sort of way, and asking trusted others for their 360 view of us.

This chapter is dedicated to bringing our attention to an array of blind spots that often derail the success, self-actualization, and even happiness of many who find themselves in leadership roles.

The checking-the-blind-spot process is never completed, in driving or in living. It requires persistent attention, as often as we're driving down the road, and as long as we breathe.

Artful Dodgers

Most of us encounter artful dodgers as we work in or volunteer for organizations.

What do artful dodgers look like? They avoid...

- Making substantive decisions.
- Owning the decisions they do make.
- Having tough conversations.
- Sharing the praise/glory/kudos.
- The messy but meaningful work that occurs on the front lines.
- Change, even when it's evident that change is needed.
- The explosion, once they've lit the fuse.

The worst of the artful dodgers are those who happen to occupy positions of leadership.

While we can't completely avoid the artful dodgers, we can most certainly avoid being like them.

Defense Shield Syndrome

We all have our defense shields. It's when our instincts tell us to BEWARE – danger or offense may be imminent. For the most part, this psychological mechanism protects us from harm, either physical or emotional. That's generally a good thing.

What is NOT a good thing is when our defense shields have to be constantly deployed in our workplaces. In order to do our best work, we should be able to spend all our energy focused on the intentional pursuit of our goals. Being constantly in defensive mode drains our energy, our time, our creativity, and our productivity. It's sort of like a slow bleed.

Leaders can create and empower workplaces free of the Defense Shield Syndrome by:

- Being persistently transparent in our actions and discussions.
- Practicing and encouraging vulnerable behaviors, by which we signal it's okay to make mistakes and to talk about them openly and to learn from them.
- Noticing and praising the effort of others consistently.
- Censuring hateful and disrespectful behavior, at any level of the organization.
- Promoting an environment of caring.
- Celebrating the good stuff, often and in many ways.
- Encouraging creativity and innovation (i.e., risk taking), in all quarters.
- Modeling honesty and trustworthiness, all the time.

It really boils down to creating an atmosphere of trust - trust that runs vertically, horizontally, obliquely, and multi-directionally throughout the organization. NOW is always a good time to start this process.

Complaints and Pushback

Leaders regularly deal with a duo of negative feedback loops. One comes in the form of complaints (usually, but not always, originating from external stakeholders). Complaints generally come from the end-users of our products or services. The other comes in the form of pushback (usually, but not always, originating from internal stakeholders). Pushback generally comes from those within the organization charged with producing/delivering our products or services.

While dealing with both is discouraging and de-energizing, leaders should view both as gifts. What? Yep, I said *GIFTS*. In both instances, the people we serve (both those external to the organization and those internal to the organization) have taken the time to provide us feedback on stuff that "ain't workin' for them," for one reason or another.

Here's how to unwrap those precious gifts:

- Thank the complainer/pushbacker for taking the time to share their insight or opinion.
- Ask them, gently, what alternatives/corrections might better serve their needs.
- LISTEN carefully to those responses and thank them again for the input.
- Bounce the suggestions off of the leadership team to determine whether those ideas have merit, and whether they fit comfortably within our cost-benefit parameters.
- Do what's best for the organization - either stick with the current plan, or alter it according to the suggestions offered by the complainers/ pushbackers.

Here's what NOT to do: Ignore the complaints and/or pushback. The cost of ignoring (and ignorance) is quite high.

Inquiring Minds

Some who hold positions of leadership spend a lot of time talking about *their* solutions. Another brand of leader spends their time listening to the possible solutions that others bring to the table.

Some who hold positions of leadership spend a lot of time issuing directives and mandates (and ultimatums). Another brand of leader directs their effort toward forging partnerships, building coalitions, and inviting others to the table.

Some who hold positions of leadership spend a lot of time chasing rainbows, crafting new flavors of the month, generating initiative tsunamis. Another brand of leader keeps their eye fully on the ball, the MAIN THING, and relentlessly tries to build effort and engagement around those pursuits.

Some who hold positions of leadership spend a lot of time avoiding the dirty work, and the customers, and the rank-and-file folks. Another brand of leader seeks out and fully engages stakeholders at all levels, learning the "business" from the ground level, and gaining perspective of the end product through the eyes of others.

Some who hold positions of leadership spend a lot of time sorting through the hard data and making decisions intended to move specific data points (e.g., profit). Another brand of leader considers the soft data *AND* the hard data, and makes decisions in the interest of affecting holistic improvement (even if incremental).

Some who hold positions of leadership spend a lot of time implementing strategies designed to promote only their organization. Another brand of leader strives to be socially responsible while remaining commercially viable.

"Another brand" for me, please.

Start Here!

"I seem to be stuck."
"It didn't go as I wanted."
"They're not willing to commit."
"The plan seems to be falling apart."

Those statements, and their many cousins, are indicative of a common psychological state - one in which we feel alone (or abandoned) in our quest.

Our reaction to being *stuck* should be one of introspection and reflection. What role are *we* playing in that stuckness?

Some good questions to begin with...

- Am I really on the right track?
- Have I invited (rather than pushed or drug) others to join in this journey?
- Is serving others a fundamental component of this project/process?
- What am *I* doing, or not doing, that's causing this stuckness?
- Are the goals I/we have set reasonable and attainable?
- Is this *thing* really worth doing?

When stuck, we ought first to look in the mirror, and ask hard questions about our own culpability.

Starting HERE – with "me" – is always the best first step.

Am I?
Am I...

- Stronger than I was yesterday (physically, emotionally, intellectually)?
- More knowledgeable than I was last week?

- More empathetic toward others than I was last month?
- More inclined to serve than I was last year?
- More loving and forgiving than at any time in my memory?
- Less judgmental than I have ever been in my life?
- Closer, somehow, to the God of my understanding than I was in the last hour?

An answer of "no" to any of those questions calls for a bit more polishing.

Time Dishonored

Time is the most precious and finite resource we have. Dishonoring the time of others is one of the most disrespectful things we can do. Yet, we see that dishonoring happen all the time, like this:

- Scheduling meetings for meetings sake, with nothing substantive to address.
- Showing up late for appointments.
- Creating and delegating "busy work," simply to fill up time.
- Engaging in long diatribes in response to straightforward questions.
- Starting meetings/events late or letting them run long.
- Interrupting one conversation (or phone call) to engage in another.
- Cold calling (showing up without an appointment).
- Being thoughtless of the time/effort/energy that another invests.
- Showing up unprepared.

Note to self: Respect the time of others as if it were my own.

Blizzard Deaths

I remember reading a short story as an elementary student about a person who died in a blizzard, only a few yards from his home. There are many similar accounts of people dying in blizzards, only feet from safety.

Just as these literal blizzard-deaths, there are also figurative ones I've seen befall leaders in organizations. The typical scenario is that circumstances/crises (i.e., blizzards) envelope these leaders, who end up being overwhelmed in the milieu. They end up losing their credibility and/or position as a result.

Two conditions portend these blizzard-deaths (both the literal kind and the figurative kind):

1) The person/leader lets go of their moorings, thus losing their bearings. In the literal deaths, they simply cannot see how close to home/safety they are because of the storm. In the figurative blizzard-death, the leader loses touch with his/her moral anchors, his/her principles, and becomes "blinded" by the overwhelming crisis.

2) In almost all these blizzard-death cases (both literal and figurative), the victim was trying to go it alone. For whatever reason, they found themselves in the midst of an overwhelming storm, without others to help, support, and guide them.

We need not allow ourselves to succumb to those two conditions. To avoid such tragedy we must constantly renew and revisit our values, as they serve as beacons that guide us in overwhelming circumstances. And, we must cling to those who love, support, and sojourn with us, as they will be the ones to help us find our way through the inevitable storms.

The sun will come out, the warmth will return, but we'll only be there to enjoy both if we bolster ourselves against blizzard-death.

Hurdles

I was a hurdler as a high school athlete. (Not a great one, mind you; just average). The thing about hurdles is that they introduce an interesting dynamic to a foot race. Hurdles present barriers that impede our progress, they "get in the way," they distract us from the business of running, they force us to be thinking about how to engage them just as much as we think about getting to the finish line. And, they can cause us to crash and burn.

In organizational work, I've seen a lot of leaders who seem to be "hurdles" for the team members.

Here are some of the ways they do that:

- They impede progress (often by making a mess of relationships).
- They get in the way (usually by requiring meaningless compliance kinds of work).
- They distract team members (by regularly calling needless meetings and demanding inconsequential activities).
- They impose themselves on the processes, procedures, systems, and meetings (as if the work is about *them*, instead of being about the organization's objectives).

Far better it is for leaders to "let go" and get out of the way of the team, and avoid being a "hurdle" to the team's progress.

The Problem

Problems happen. They are a part of life. They are most certainly a part of organizational life.

So, how do we deal with problems? Sometimes we pretend the problems don't exist and hope they magically disappear. This approach almost always bites us on the bum. Ignored problems have an insidious nature to them. Ignoring problems is bad business.

Sometimes we are so distracted with our busyness that we fail to notice a problem. By the time it shows up on our radar screen it has moved from being a manageable issue to a downright dastardly situation. Not noticing and being distracted by inconsequential stuff is our downfall on this front. Obliviousness is fertile ground for problem propagation.

Sometimes we are aware of the problem but feel that we are either incapable of interdicting it or that others can/will take care of it. We watch the problem evolve, but remain silent, in hopes that it will get handled by others. Our failure to openly identify it as a problem from the outset almost always becomes a point of regret for us. Avoidance won't make problems disappear.

Sometimes we notice problems arising and quickly and openly discuss it with those who are involved or who will be involved. We ask important questions about the root causes of the problem (without issuing indictments). We seek to clarify if and how the problem, if unresolved, will impact the health and wellbeing of the organization (and the team players, as individuals). We ask for possible solutions from the team players in and around the center of the "storm." We support, facilitate, cheer, resource the problem solvers. Transparent and attentive engagement with problems is good practice.

The choice does seem clear, no?

Shooting the Cat

Early in my career as an educator I taught several children from one family that truly lived "out in the sticks." The children of this family would often grace us with interesting stories of their unique country lifestyle.

The kids in this family were at the table eating one evening when the mother issued a directive: "Get the cat off the table."

The kids kept eating, presumably so engrossed in their meal that they didn't hear their mother. A few minutes later, the mom seconded her directive: "I said get the cat off the table!" Again her demand went unheeded.

Soon thereafter a shotgun blast interrupted the feast. Kids ducked for cover, chairs clattered to the floor. As the smoke cleared and the ringing in their ears began to dissipate, mom lowered the gun barrel and issued this declaration: "I told you to get the &@%# cat off the table." She then calmly left the room to re-rack the shotgun.

I've thought of that story often with respect to the exercise of leadership. To be sure, folks need to know that we mean what we say. However, it is much wiser to outline our expectations (as this mother did) AND define clearly the consequences for the failure to meet those expectations (which this mother did not).

While shooting the cat achieved her objective and focused the whole team on her expectations, the collateral damage (and I'm sure there was plenty) was probably not worth her failure to communicate the possible consequences.

Mediocrity's Child

Mediocrity begets mediocrity. How often have we heard leaders of organizations rail about lack of intensity, anemic motivation, and poor performance. Almost always, their ire is directed at *others*!

Could it be that, if an environment of mediocrity exists, we as leaders have created the conditions that promote (or worse, incentivize) such behaviors? Moreover, we must consider the possibility that the egregious behaviors seen in others are simply reflections (or offspring) of our own.

If mediocrity begets mediocrity (and I think it does) then we must look in the mirror FIRST to explore its roots.

Hunkering Down = Death

One of the classic defensive measures in animals is to "hunker down." It is defensive in nature because it is designed to protect the present status, to avoid risk, to thwart or to stall.

Many organizations choose to hunker down to protect market share, or to "not rock the boat," or to preserve the current organizational structure and/ or dynamics.

This digging-in effect is usually viewed as a protective measure, and quite frequently its deployment is meant to protect jobs, vendors, employees, pensions, etc.

Rarely is hunkering down utilized in the interest of the customer's needs. Worth noting is the fact that without customers we've got a bit of a problem.

Diagnosisaster

As a high school athlete I learned a powerful lesson about the potential disasters that befall those who diagnose problems in too big a hurry. During a high school football game one of my teammates (I'll call him Jack) got his "bell rung" (these days, they call those concussions) and was laying flat on his back on the field, out like a light. Those were the days before schools had athletic trainers so it always fell to one of the assistant coaches to be the resident "medic." On our team, that person was Coach B.

Coach B rushed from the sidelines, medical kit in hand, to quickly discern what the problem was with Jack. Breathing? Yep. Broken bones? Nope. Bleeding profusely? Nope. Lucid? Not a chance. Communicable? Not. Diagnosis: Knocked cuckoo and out cold.

Once Coach B had made his expert diagnosis he quickly broke open an ammonia capsule (aka, "am caps"). Ammonia capsules broken apart release an aroma that will very nearly raise the dead. Coach B waved am cap #1 under Jack's nose. This act should've given Jack a jolt similar to that of administering electrical defibrillation. However, Jack remained motionless.

Coach B tossed that am cap over his shoulder and grabbed another, and quickly cracked it open. He waved am cap #2 under Jack's nose. Still no visible impact from a treatment that should have brought Jack from prone to sprinting in less than a second. Nada.

Coach B then made his second quick diagnosis of the evening. He deduced that the am caps themselves must be faulty or out-of-date, thus not having their usual punch. Coach B then grabbed am cap #3, cracked it open and inhaled its ingredients deeply into his own lungs.

Now our team had *TWO* folks in supine position on the field - Jack *and* Coach B.

I've heard it said over the years that students in medical school are taught to respond to all emergencies in a leisurely fashion. After watching Coach B's frantic and hurried diagnoses that night on the gridiron, I learned that lesson early on. When things are the craziest, it pays to slow the pace just a bit...

Dime-a-Dozen

As Moe (my lovely wife) and I were raising our daughters, we would often get into conversations with them about potential. Over many dinners we would dialogue about getting the most of the gifts God has given us. As educators, my wife and I could cite example after example of former students who seemed to bleed their gifts for every last drop. Of course, we could also recount a rather large number who never seemed to come close to reaching their potential.

The message we repeatedly communicated to our daughters was this: People with potential are a dime a dozen.

EVERYONE has potential. Decisions about who to marry, who to go into business with, who to spend your time with, who to work with, who to depend on in a crunch should *never* be made based on potential. Potential is meaningless, unless developed and leveraged with fervor.

The folks who actually optimize their potential, who fully activate their gifts, who develop their talents with zeal – they're the ones who should get the lion's share of our personal investments of attention, time, cooperation, and partnership.

Why? Because people with potential really are a dime per dozen.

Perturburances

I have been blessed to work with/for/around some amazingly talented people over the years. One trend I've noticed is that many extremely talented people are what we sometimes describe as "high-maintenance." While they may be masterful organizers, musicians, thinkers, gitter-doners, etc., many also possess some interesting quirks (often closely akin to passionate obsessions). I have come to think of these folks as "perturberances" (yep, another word I made up).

As an organizational leader, I've frequently found myself supervising said perturberances. And, I often find myself mentoring young organizational leaders, who find *themselves* supervising said perturberances. Not a few organizational leaders get distracted by those highly talented, but disturbance-causing people (i.e., the perturberances). Some mentees share those frustrations with me, seeking a solution to the heartburn the perturberances cause. And they *think* they want to control or manage those disturbance creators. I used to suffer from the same illusions. The all too often end result is that the talent walks.

Our teams *NEED* talent. No team can have too much talent. However, the fact is that talent can work just about anywhere talent wants to. Tolerating a bit of perturberance on a team is worth it to salvage the talent, and the team's performance and its innovativeness. Learning to live with the perturburances is an important step in our growth as leaders. Admittedly, care must be taken to monitor team chemistry closely. There can (and sometimes does) come a point at which the team can no longer abide the idiosyncrasies of the perturberances, and becomes dysfunctional. At that point, a parting of ways may be necessary. However, that is not the typical circumstance.

I have come to believe (rather firmly) that organizational environments that foster a culture of mastery, purpose, and autonomy (see Pink, 2012) are the ones that best accommodate the perturberance types. What happens too often is that cultural norms that insist on consistency, compliance, think-alike-ness, talk-alike-ness, look-alike-ness also have the tendency to manifest mediocre kinds of perform-alike-ness. That is not the kind of team I want to be on, or lead.

Over the years I've learned to enjoy working with the perturberances, despite the heartburn they sometimes cause. What they add to the organization, generally, far outweighs any dissonance they cause. You can send your perturbances my way if you get tired of them.

Loyalty

For years I've heard leaders pontificate on the topic of loyalty. Loyalty is usually espoused as a virtue, to be coveted in organizational behavior. Generally, I have seen it in organizational literature and heard it in the language of leaders trying to muster support, and usually, acquiescence. That appeal (often packaged as an implied demand) for loyalty has never resonated with me.

Here's why: Loyalty to an organization or to a person is something that has to be *earned*. Not coerced. Not requested. Not demanded. Not artificially fabricated.

Folks are loyal to organizations because they believe in the vision/mission that the organization espouses or represents. Folks are loyal to other people because of the integrity, credibility, and trustworthiness those others embody. Speechifying about loyalty does nothing to foster loyalty. In fact, it seems to do quite the contrary.

Fence Moving

Horn (2015) offers advice to those of us who find ourselves in roles of leadership: "Don't go moving fences until you know why they're there."

This admonition rings true with me from my experience as an organizational leader. Fences exist for numerous reasons: boundary setting, to hold something in, to keep something out, warning, aesthetics, protection. Boundaries, parameters, beliefs, cultures – *FENCES* – are almost always the result of hours, days, months, and years of labor and negotiated agreements.

"Fences" sometimes *need* to moved. Before that takes place, however, we ought to take careful assessment of the history and agreements that forged their original placement and the beneficiaries of their current location.

Only after we have a full understanding of the current placement history, and only after we have made a sound case for changing the location, should we engage in "fence moving."

Pharaoh Syndrome

In 1956 Paramount Pictures released a classic movie titled "The Ten Commandments." It is the biblical story of Moses (played by Charlton Heston) leading the children of Israel out of their long-term bondage in Egypt, which was ruled by Pharaoh (played by Yul Brynner).

A powerful leadership lesson for me from that movie is the futility of what I call the "Pharaoh Syndrome" of leadership – the belief that, based on formal authority, one can simply speak problems out of existence. It is self-deception at its finest. Moses repeatedly confronted Pharaoh with news of impending catastrophe unless Pharaoh released the Jewish people from bondage.

Pharaoh's response each and every time was to defiantly refuse. Each obstinate refusal was punctuated by these words, "So let it be written, so let it be done!"

Pharaoh suffered from the *illusion* that the power of his position would allow him to speak problems out of existence. He believed that a wave of the scepter would eliminate the issue. Yet, the locusts came anyway, the frogs invaded anyway, the plagues progressed anyway, the spirit of death visited Egypt nonetheless.

Pharaoh learned some hard lessons about the limits of his authority. Those of us in leadership positions (whether bosses, parents, captains, or preachers) would be wise to learn from Pharaoh's mistakes.

Rattlesnakes

When I teach aspiring school principals, I share what I call "Rattlesnake Alerts." These scenarios consist of the unexpected challenges and disasters that present themselves to principals every working day of every school year. It's the kind of stuff you don't find in textbooks, the bombshells that walk in the door on you without warning. To be certain, those kinds of "rattlesnakes" do not visit only school principals; they happen to anyone who finds themselves in leadership roles.

Through the process of dissecting and analyzing these catastrophes it is my intention to guide emerging leaders in developing a set of psychological, intellectual, and emotional skills which will help them successfully manage crises and lead others effectively "through the storm."

The concept of the Rattlesnake Alert took on new meaning for me when my youngest daughter was bitten by a real rattlesnake a few years ago. After a life-flight on a helicopter, three days in intensive care, one more day in the hospital, and months of convalescence, she still, now years later, suffers residual effects of the powerful venom. The amount of pain was remarkable. The psychological and emotional impact was equally challenging.

Watching my daughter cope with the derivative effects of a rattlesnake bite reinforced in my mind several things about leadership (and crisis) preparedness:

1) Those of us in leadership roles must always be duly diligent and alert to the "rattlesnakes" that live among us. Even when others are not.

2) Rattlesnake bites (and crises) always have rippling effects, even beyond those who are bitten.

3) Thoughtful preparation for possible emergencies, upheavals, disasters, crises can make a profound difference on the response, survival and recovery of the individual and/or the group.

4) Knowing where and from whom to seek support in the aftermath of a crisis (or rattlesnake bite) has great bearing on how quickly and how well recuperation occurs. Having committed and knowledgeable mentors/responders is profoundly important.

5) Thoughtful reflection can enhance our ability to weather the next storm (which is always looming on the horizon). Effective leaders must take the initiative to engage in this reflective process with teams.

6) Killing the rattlesnake does not alleviate the need for preparedness. There are always more rattlesnakes in the vicinity. They live here, too.

Leadership is never needed more than when the organization, the team, the family, the relationship is under duress.

Diverse-iverse

Consider the richest and most vibrant environments of our planet or universe – tropical rain forests, the oceans, the African Serengeti ecosystem, emerging galaxies... In each we find vast amounts of diversity. That diversity may be in the form of an abundance of microbial life, huge volumes of plant life, amazing and complex webs of animal life, and/or a tremendous interplay of physical/chemical interactions.

Likewise, the richest intellectual, physical, and spiritual human environments consist of tremendous diversity. The world in which we live is an overwhelming mish-mash of *difference* (i.e., uniqueness, diversity). Pretending that we can better ourselves or our organizations by serving all those "others" in a one-size-fits-all, homogenous way necessarily means that we have excluded (discriminated against?) a far greater number than we include. Succumbing to the dogma of homogeneity makes us less instead of more, both personally and organizationally.

This diversity and interconnectedness has great implications for us, our lives, and our work. Being unaware of, or worse, ignoring, that dynamic diversity is a blind spot no leader can afford to disregard.

9

Organizational Fitness: Raising the Cultural Average

"I came to see, in my time at IBM, that culture isn't just one aspect of the game, it is the game. In the end, an organization is nothing more than the collective capacity of its people to create value."

- Louis Gerstner, IBM

Culture - The DNA of the Organization

The culture of an organization is a complex amalgam of variables that include beliefs, norms, values, symbols, rituals, celebrations, customs, heroes, artifacts, stories, and history. Every group of humans on the planet has an organizational culture, whether the group is as small as a family or as large as a nation. We can think of culture as the DNA of an organization – the most fundamental building blocks that make the organization what it is. Culture drives the ways of thinking and ways of behaving among the organization's members.

What about climate? Climate is the tangible manifestation of the culture. It is the look, feel, and smell of how the organization presents itself to the outside observer. In terms of businesses or schools, we can "feel" the climate when we walk through the front doors. There is no question that the climate on a Southwest Airlines flight is different from that of an American Airlines flight. Both are the outward manifestations of their respective organizational cultures.

Organizations, by their very definition, are composed of collections of humans. As we consider the concept of organizational fitness, please think of fitness in holistic terms, not in just physical terms. Fitness is the symbiotic and cumulative health of *all* the systems within the body. The same line of thinking applies to the fitness of organizations. Thus, the fitness of an organization is in many ways a derivative of the fitness of each of its individual members. Imagine trying to move an organization to a high level of fitness if most of its members are unfit. Not likely.

Organizational fitness exists in the same three domains as personal fitness: emotional/spiritual, intellectual, and physical (discussed in Chapter 3). Thus, attention must be focused on how the culture of the organization values each domain, and attends to the health of each. Just as individual humans grow, thrive, and prosper as their needs (on Maslow's hierarchy) are met, so is organizational acuity driven by its needs-met status. Earley and Mosakowski (2004) speak of cultural intelligence – the ability to perceive how the head, body, and heart work together. Healthy and robust organizations exemplify this whole-health sort of thinking.

We read and hear a lot about changing the culture of an organization. Sometimes it's framed as displacing one culture and replacing it with a new one. My work in organizations has led me to believe that culture is very much like human dispositions. Just as our personal dispositions spring from a combination of our genes and environmental factors, so is organizational culture a natural outgrowth of similar seminal elements. Thus, for those of us who live and work in organizations, our focus should more realistically be aimed at *influencing*, or *shaping*, the culture. There are far too many mediating variables to completely throw out one culture and replace it with another – as if we could, anyway. Please recall the marshmallow analogy in Chapter 4; organizational culture tends toward its dispositional state.

This chapter will pose ideas and concepts meant to bump your thinking toward ways of influencing organizational culture in positive, powerful, and lasting ways.

The Cultural Average

To achieve "average" status, the only thing required of us is to keep breathing. To pursue, or simply meander toward, mediocrity seems inane, if not downright insane. To live *consequential* lives is within the reach of each one of us, regardless of our station in life.

From a leadership perspective, there is a similar mindset of organizational mediocrity. If we preach, incentivize, and promote conformity in our organization, we are essentially encouraging a race to the bottom — to the bottom of effort, to the bottom of creativity, to the bottom of risk-taking, to the bottom of innovation, to the bottom of performance.

Never do all the members of an organization subscribe to and strictly abide by every organizational tenet. There is an average at work. Ken Wilber (1996) asserts that every group of people (e.g., families, churches, schools, businesses, nations) has a "cultural average." He suggests that the "culture" of a people-group is simply the mean of their beliefs, values, mores, and behavioral norms. If we accept his argument, then that implies that about half the folks in the people-group, think, live, and behave in ways that exceed

the cultural average. Likewise, about half think, live, and behave in ways that are below that cultural average.

Leaders of groups (whether ski clubs, Sunday school classes, or unions) must find ways to raise the cultural average. Concrete steps can be taken to affect that raising, and they come in a thousand possibilities.

Shared organizational goals should be the driver of our attempts to raise the cultural average, not shared protocols, procedures, haircuts, etc. Unless, of course, conformity and mediocrity are our desired outcomes.

Culture Work

Much of the organizational literature provides guidance on "building" or "creating" culture. We really can't "create" culture. Culture simply *exists*, in all organizations. It is an organic outgrowth of the dynamics and interactions of the members of the organization, all of which are influenced by the collective attitudes and practices of the organization's members. And, culture is implicitly tied up with the history of the group. It is not only a function of the current membership.

Because culture is very much a self-organizing system, we do not have the power to simply conjure up the culture we desire. The idea that we get to create the culture we want is a notion that is *WAY* too simplified for the realities on the ground, and it could even be described as downright naïve.

What we can (and should) do is purposefully and positively *influence* the culture of our organization (whether it be a family, a softball team, a yoga class, a business, or a school). How? By our attitudes, our acts of commission, our acts of omission, and our treatment of others. EVERY person within an organization exercises *some* influence on the culture of the organization. And, the degree of influence is not necessarily tied to where one lies in the organizational hierarchy.

So, how can we influence our organization's culture in positive ways? One way is to insist on and model respectful treatment of ALL others. Another powerful strategy is to notice and celebrate behaviors consistent with the organizational culture we desire. We can also be extremely purposeful when the opportunity to add new organizational members presents itself. We can design recruitment and induction processes that will unveil candidates with the attributes that will positively influence the organization. To quote Todd Whitaker (2012), "Don't hire the people that fit your organization; hire the people you want your organization to become." Another powerful culture influencer is to communicate often and in many ways the kinds of behaviors, beliefs, and values that represent the desired cultural norms. Folks will both over- and under-achieve those desired norms, but they'll at least be aware of the aspirations if the desired outcomes are clearly articulated.

Important to remember is that organizational culture is dynamic in nature. It is constantly being flexed, stretched, and altered by changes in membership, by changes in circumstances, and by changes in the external variables. The only thing we can control is how we act and react. However, we should be very cognizant of the fact that each of those actions and reactions will influence the culture of our organization.

Fun Team

I've been blessed to be a part of all kinds of teams over the years, from athletic teams to work teams to teams of volunteers. Some of those teams have been simply marvelous to "play" on. Others, not so much.

So, what were the differences? All had talented, smart and capable folks on them. What made some of them much more enjoyable, fulfilling, usually more successful, and self-actualizing?

- They had a clear vision of the outcomes they were pursuing.
- Their leaders were others-centered people, interested in team objectives, not personal accolades.
- They pursued challenging goals and tackled tough problems.
- Team members gave more than they took, and didn't "skate."
- Tussles, conflicts, and debates were civil, respectful, and centered on team (not personal) objectives.
- Trust between and among team members was pervasive.
- The collective focus permeated the team's interactions and created synergy.
- Team members understood that effort, failure, laughter, struggle, blood, sweat, and tears were necessary ingredients in the process.

- They were adaptable, fluid, and dynamic in response to the conditions/contexts.
- They ran their course, then ended (they didn't artificially try to extend the life cycle of the team).

What great fun it is to play on those kinds of teams!

Habits, Behaviors, and Beliefs

There's a strong relationship between habits, behaviors, and beliefs. Beliefs are the foundational values we espouse to be the drivers of our lives, and of our organizations. "Espoused" is the stuff we *say* we believe, not necessarily the stuff we act upon. For instance, it is quite common for people to declare themselves followers of one religious faith or another, but their actions betray a lack of conviction.

Behaviors are the truest manifestations of our commitments. They are the "proof in the pudding," so to speak. If we are persnickety about our clothes, then it is evident in the polish of our shoes, the fit of our shirts, the coordination of our ensembles. If we are passionate about serving others, then it shows in the way we treat them, the effort we invest in assisting them, and the responsiveness they find in us when they seek our help.

Even though our behaviors are the most reliable indicators of our beliefs, it's our *HABITS* that drive our behaviors. The little habits we build into our lives - our manners (or lack thereof), the way we spend our daily time, the act of suspending other tasks to focus on the person we are engaged with, the choice of foods we consume each day, the kinds of blogs/books/articles we read - are the drivers of our behaviors, and thus, the enforcers and reinforcers of our beliefs.

Our beliefs are evidenced in our behaviors, our behaviors are evidenced in our habits.

Habits are hard to initiate, and harder to change. But if we want to truly affect some kind of serious change in our behaviors, then the place to start is with altering the habits that drive those behaviors. This is true both in our personal lives and in the organizations to which we belong.

Fixing

I used to think I could *fix* things. No more. Through years of trying, I have learned that I never have quite enough knowledge of the big picture to fix things up. There always seem to be pieces of the puzzle that are not on the table for me.

When I presumed that I was the one to fix things it seemed to give others permission to "stand down" and happily let me slave away at the fixing. At times, when I imposed my fixing propensities on a situation (or person), others felt diminished; they resented my arrogance and/or imposition. Almost always, inclinations to be a fixer triggered from me directives, mandates, mind-numbing procedures, ultimatums, and healthy doses of ill will.

The result? I never seemed to fix what I deemed to be fix-worthy.

I finally learned that my job is not to be the fixer. My job is to engage with others, assess our level of progress, discuss what a better future might look like, then work together toward that end. It's not so much about fixing what (or who) I perceive is broken as it is about positing a better future and seizing the opportunities to achieve it.

Are things (and people) still broken? Sure. There will always be broken stuff (and people).

Our energy is best used, however, to create the conditions in which *WE* can make it better. In the case of people, it's about creating the conditions in which they can see and make a better future for themselves. That is the work of culture shaping. That work is just as hard as fixing, but not nearly as frustrating.

Covenant, Not Contract

Doug Christensen (2014) describes the relationship between the leaders of an organization and its membership as a "covenant, not a contract." When a relationship is framed in terms of a contract, then several associated words/phrases come to mind: legally binding, expectations, requirements, obligation, enforceability, and/or arrangement.

I suppose all those words are important in assuring that an organization is positioning itself to pursue its stated goals; however, they are rather legalistic and compliance-driven. External rewards and punishments seem to be the drivers.

Covenant, on the other hand, has a very different ring to it. Words/phrases I associate with covenant are: sacred bond, investment, collective endeavor, affiliation, pledge, and/or commitment.

The best organizations (the kind I want to be a part of) are the ones that are built on the solid foundation of mutual respect, the pursuit of worthy goals that go beyond making a profit or simply doing some job, and the synergy that springs from a collective commitment to achieving those worthy goals.

Our choice is between collaboration and enthusiastic engagement, OR legalistic and compliance-premised participation.

"Covenant." The word implies an intrinsically motivated investment of body, mind, *AND* spirit. There seems to be a holiness that undergirds such a partnership. There are significant implications for raising the cultural average when we think and act in terms of covenant, rather than contract.

Simple Rules

I was watching a television documentary about 15 years ago that moved me deeply. A family in the northern United States had adopted not one, not two, but 12 children. Moreover, every one of those dozen children had some kind of challenging physical or cognitive life-limiting condition. One was blind, another had cerebral palsy, a third had deformed arms, etc. These special needs children ranged in ages from one to 18.

The journalist in the documentary was interviewing the parents and all the children who were capable of responding. His questions probed the motivations of the parents, the systems used by the family to function, and the dynamics of living in such a challenging environment.

Two of those responses continue to linger with me. When the journalist asked the parents Why? - Why so many? Why such challenging children? Why such a broad age range? Why such diversity of needs? – the parents' response was simple and heart-warming: "We've got more than enough love to share." Wow!

Secondly, the journalist queried the 18-year-old boy with Down Syndrome, positing that living in such a diverse and challenging family dynamic must require an elaborate set of interactional rules and protocols. The young man simply shook his head and said, "No, sir, we just have one rule in our family." Puzzled, the journalist asked what such a powerful rule might be. The boy's response: "If you're making your brothers and sisters cry, then you're probably doing something wrong."

I invite you to consider the possibilities if we were to apply both of these simple axioms to our personal, professional, and organizational lives:

1) We can never give away too much love. The more we give, the more we have to share.
2) If we're making our brothers and sisters cry, we're probably doing something wrong.

These are powerful tenets by which to influence organizational culture.

Ways of Thinking, Ways of Behaving

Organizational culture is very much a function of ways of thinking and ways of behaving, even more so than ways of knowing and ways of doing.

Standardationists (yep, it's a made-up word) promote the reduction of variability in the organizational endeavor, as if it were a manufacturing assembly line. They proclaim that eliminating variability in the delivery of goods or services is the scalable factor for eventual organizational success. This might be true if one's customers are machines or robots. But, they aren't. People are humans (or humans are people). What counts for each of us as individuals is the level and quality of the engagement with the organization.

Thus, we should strive as leaders to optimize the engagement factor for each customer, rather than the more easily measurable elements like response time, portion sizes, warranties and so forth. The health of the organizational culture is most evident in person-to-person interactions.

From Where We Are to Where We Wanna Be

The difference in where our organization is today and where we aspire for it to be in the future is directly proportional to the quality of the people who are members of that organization. As leaders, then, we are compelled to somehow increase the quality and performance of the organization (in Ken Wilber terms, the "cultural average"). But how?

The surest and fastest way to increase the cultural average is to attract, hire, and retain talented, right-thinking, right-behaving members to our organization. If we hire the right people, we need little else. But we do need *something* else, and that *something* is a healthy organizational culture.

Not only must our organization learn how to attract talent, it must also know how to breed talent. Beyond that, in order to retain and incubate talent, we must strive daily to create the conditions in which talent wants to work/live/play (that's the "retain" part of the equation). Why? Because one of the surest realities is that talented folks can pretty much work wherever they want to. Thus, we must ask ourselves daily the following question: Why would talented people choose to be part of our organization? Our challenge then, in terms of organizational culture, is to create and sustain environmental conditions favorable to attracting and holding talent.

Leaders who view the future of their organizations in terms of profit/loss, market share, enrollment, brand recognition, test scores, deals closed, cars sold, etc., are simply deceiving themselves. The wisest leaders invest fully and often in the growth of the members of the organization. The most talented organizations figure out ways to tap the varied talents of ALL their members.

Our people *ARE* our brand. We must be constantly aware of what messages that brand conveys, to those inside the organization as well as to those outside.

Mentoring

Leadership development is not the responsibility of the human resource department. It is the responsibility of the current leadership team. We cannot abdicate the job of building the capacity of our organization's next generation of leaders, whether that organization is our family, our church, our charitable organization, our business, or our nation.

The work of attending to leadership succession is not only a fundamental responsibility of current leaders, it is also an opportunity to shape the future culture and impact of our organization. And, since most of us belong to multiple organizations that are nested within one another, that overlap with one another, that are intertwined with one another, and that are juxtaposed to one another, that development of future leaders is significant and consequential.

Thus, the very intentional and deliberate development of our children, our volunteers, our teachers, our sergeants, our sales people, our _____
(fill in the blank), will make all the difference in the world for them as individuals, and for the future of our organizations, and to the world that will evolve beyond our passing.

185

Notice that the root word of succession is *success*. Time to reflect, revisit, and revise our role in this critically important process.

Mentors

Having a respected and willing mentor is critical to our success, whether we are trying to learn the craft of fly fishing, painting, accounting, management, farming, yoga, leadership or any other endeavor that requires the acquisition of significant skills and knowledge. Quality mentors can make our learning meaningful, relevant, seamless, and relatively disaster free (not mistake free).

Here are some of the attributes of a quality mentor:

- They truly believe in and desire to see the mentee succeed.
- They do the work of mentoring for the service, not for the money.
- They are accessible NOW (not two days from now or next week or next month).
- They connect seamlessly with the mentee, face-to-face, by phone, email, texting, etc.
- They share their learning regularly, as well as respond to queries.
- They teach ways of thinking, not procedures.
- They diligently work to build floors under others, rather than ceilings over them.
- They constantly help mentees toggle from the BIG picture to the tiniest details.
- They are honest, but not hurtful, in their feedback.
- They "coach on the fly" rather than engage in infrequent yet voluminous exchanges.
- They ask LOTS of good questions.
- They listen powerfully.

Mentorship is "circular" in nature. Not only do we need mentors, we need to be mentors, too. It is not unlike the duality many of us experience in being both parent and child at the same time. In attempting to be better at both of those roles, we develop a deeper understanding of each.

Powerful mentoring is a pivotal act of culture shaping.

Shaping

We are constantly being shaped (i.e., influenced) by the thinking, the behavior, the beliefs, and the modeling of valued others in our lives. However, we are, at the same time, shaping (i.e., influencing) those around us.

Shaping is a recursive exercise. Our thinking, our espoused beliefs, our enacted beliefs, our biases, our level of enthusiasm, our service orientation, our etiquette, our speech, our empathy, our zealous pursuits, etc., are constantly impacting and "moving" those within our sphere of influence.

With that in mind, consider this question: Am I shaping others in a way that improves their lives?

That question has everything to do with raising the cultural average.

Talent Boosters

A fundamental role of leadership (whether it be as a parent, a teacher, a manager, a coach, or a business owner) is to facilitate the development of the talent on our team. Talent is not created by us; rather, it is a gift of birth, which comes in a billion varieties. Every team member has *some* kind of talent, and many of them have multiple talents.

As leaders we must:

1) Identify the talent(s) of those within our circle of influence.
2) Help those folks understand, and understand the value of, their precious gifts.

3) Create the conditions in which our teammates can exercise their talents.
4) Encourage a continuous "polishing" of those talents.
5) Celebrate and affirm the successful use of those talents.

In effect, we should be talent boosters. The culture we desire depends on it.

Strength
Diversity adds richness - diversity in thought, age, maturity, skin color, expertise, gifts, political leanings, and in religious inclinations.

Diversity does not necessarily imply strength. Strength comes from unity, unified effort around a noble and worthy vision.

Wise leaders encourage us to celebrate our diversity and teach us how to respect our differences. They also help us see the better future we can create through coalescing around a powerful vision.

The Best We've Got
Many years I heard an iconic NCAA Division I football coach talking about the problem of negativism among his assistant coaches. This coach, who had won several national titles and whose teams were always highly ranked, described an environment in which the assistant coaches persistently criticized the players, both in their presence and out.

Remember, this is a top tier Division I NCAA program that recruits *and gets* pretty much whatever players they want. As I heard the coach speaking I was wondering how in the world there could be such negativity toward what was unquestionably one of the best stable of players in the nation.

The coach described how he placed a sign above the coaches' office door, which stated the following: "Don't bitch about the players; they're the best ones we've got!"

We see that same dynamic of negativity in many organizational settings - from parents toward their children, from principals toward their teachers, from foremen toward their work crews, from executives toward their leadership team. Complaining, demeaning, diminishing, debasing, disparaging - whether publicly or privately - never pays dividends. Why would those in leadership roles insult the very people upon whom their futures depend?

A better way...

- Assess the root causes of poor performance rather than attacking team members on a personal level.
- Collaboratively set very clear goals and pursue them relentlessly, *together*.
- Strive diligently to craft a culture of continuous improvement, in which every "player" is encouraged and expected to get better everyday, and to help others get better everyday.
- Recognize and celebrate the "wins" ritually, and talk honestly (not meanly) about the next steps needed to rectify the "losses."
- Frame all conversations in the we-us context, not the me-you or us-them context.

When the team fails, the whole team fails. One of our primary jobs as leaders is to build others up, so that we *all* experience success.

Don't bitch about the players (or the boss); they're the best ones we've got. And, it's a powerful tool for raising the cultural average.

Human Capital as Life Flow
Human capital, by definition, is the sum effect that humans contribute to the productivity of an organization - things like skills, knowledge, habits, and social and interpersonal prowess. Usually, human capital is discussed as just one mechanical piece in the larger organizational structure. The organization is thought of in terms of parts and pieces - schedules, supply lines, organizational

charts, human capital, infrastructure, strategic plans, capital outlay, etc. That is the wrong way to think about it.

Oft forgotten (or ignored, or dismissed) is the fact that organizations are *systems*, much like the human body is a system. And, it's the humans within the system that give it life, much like the blood in a human body. The humans in the system flow in and out and between and among all the other "pieces" (the cells/organs/systems of the organization). In the process, they transport the nutrients, the oxygen, the disease fighters, and, yes, even the toxins.

In that respect, the organization's health is not only the direct beneficiary of the human capital, the human capital is the direct beneficiary of the collective, systemic wellness of the organization. This symbiotic relationship is what we often call "culture." The humans feed the culture, which feeds the humans, which feeds the culture, which...

Wellness (either as individuals or organizations) is a physical thing, an intellectual thing, and an emotional/spiritual thing. Sound familiar? All in one, all at once, all intertwined. It is the sum of the knowledge, the skills, the thinking processes, the physical fitness, the peace, the love, the rituals, the nutrition, the learning, the dispositions, the improvements, the interactions,... of the WHOLE.

ONLY when the humans in the organization are holistically healthy and well can the organization be fully healthy and well. When this duality exists, the culture of the organization synergistically fosters healthier humans. It's a reciprocal and recursive dynamic. A fundamental role of leaders is to attend to the health and wellbeing of both.

Positive Environs

Environment and culture are virtually indistinguishable components of the organization. Wise leaders are astutely aware of the environmental dynamics, while persistently tweaking specific factors in the interest of culture shaping. They understand that the healthiest environments afford emotional and psychological safety for all.

According to Covey (2004), there are five cancerous cultural behaviors in organizations: criticizing, complaining, comparing, competing, and contending. The best way to deal with these elements of cultural toxicity is to create environments of transparency, free flow of information (vertically, horizontally, internally, and externally), and a hierarchical flattening of the organization so that "privileged" classes do not exist. Flattening the organization has the same effect as exercise on the human body; it tends to "align" the systems into more efficient, effective, seamless performance.

Negative organizational environments seem to grow and prosper under their own steam. It's almost like they have the ability to metastasize. Negative energy serves as a constant draw-down force, much like gravity. Positive environments, however, require our constant attention. It is a never-ending job to make the positive offset the negative. But, Pollyanna mentality won't get the job done.

Positive behavior/thinking has to be defined, incentivized, praised, recognized, and practiced relentlessly. And, because it doesn't seem to be the natural disposition; the habit of positivity must be learned, trained, and reinforced. This is the work of leadership. The work of fostering positivity in the work environment is similar to the practice of maintaining fitness for ourselves. We never "get there." It requires our constant, daily, disciplined attention to maintain wellness in our body, mind, and spirit.

Same goes for the places in which we work. And, regardless of the position we hold within an organization, we actually *ARE* daily engaging in practices that make that environment healthier, more positive, more fit .... or not.

Mitigate the Madness

Nobody likes to work in a toxic work environment. There are a lot of variables that can cause the workplace to feel de-energizing, frustrating, and/or down-right oppressive. Unfortunately, "the boss" is somehow implicated in many of those toxifying possibilities.

So, how can leaders act and behave in ways that mitigate such madness?

- Actually care for the people who work with us. Get to know them, what their interests are, what they struggle with, what makes 'em tick. It's okay to care. Really.
- Neither be a jerk, nor tolerate jerks as team members (for any length of time).
- In as many ways as possible, make the workplace as pleasant and enjoyable as we can. Fun is literally like medicine (both personally and organizationally).
- Ask for the help and the thinking of team members as often as possible. Few things energize us as much as when we feel valued.
- Treat everyone respectfully (whether they've earned our respect or not). The collateral damage that accrues when leaders mistreat *anyone* (deserving or not) is incalculable.
- Understand that attitudes are contagious, in direct proportion to the level of authority.
- When problems arise, tackle them as opportunities first. Once resolved, then reflect on the root causes. Jumping to conclusions and laying blame as an initial reaction will cause others to head for the exits.
- Be accessible and be responsive.
- Paint desired outcomes as clearly as possible, but resist prescribing the pathways toward achievement. Allow as much autonomy as we can stand (and just a tad bit more).
- Notice. Notice! NOTICE! Notice good work and acknowledge it relentlessly.

TRUST

Without trust there is no organizational fitness. The ability to engender and foster the trust of others is critical for leaders and their subsequent effectiveness. S. M. R. Covey (2006) notes that organizations pay a high price for allowing and/or promulgating low-trust environments. He calls this a "tax" on the organization and describes seven common elements indicative of such organizations: redundancy, bureaucracy, politics, disengagement, turnover, churn, and fraud. Covey also describes the dividends of high-trust organizational environments as increased value, accelerated growth, enhanced innovation, improved collaboration, stronger partnering, better execution, and heightened loyalty.

Another way to think of trust is in terms of safety. Without safety, both emotional and physical, there can be no significant level of trust. Why? Because our evolutionary psychology dictates such – we cannot and will not feel safe with those (and in environments in which) we do not trust.

Trust can be thought of as the gold-standard health marker of organizations, one which wise leaders should be constantly monitoring. We can monitor trust levels through constant dipsticking, engaging in an observant and persistent process similar to the medical physical (rather than the after-the-fact autopsy).

In most instances, strong relationships must be the precursor to real trust. Relationships can be parallel, adversarial, competitive, collegial, or congenial. Obviously some of those varieties are healthier than others. One way or the other, strong and positive relationships are key to organizational fitness.

The foundational component in establishing strong relationships is respectful interactions. Each and every member in the organization should be able to expect to be treated in respectful and dignified ways.

Authenticity or Integrity

Authenticity suggests that we are what we proclaim to be. It belies a sense of genuineness about us. Those are good things. Authenticity, however, is subject to perception, to image management, to illusion. It is not at all difficult to *appear* authentic, yet not be. This machination is successfully deployed rather frequently by politicians, con artists, salesmen, and a large number of organizational leaders.

Integrity, on the other hand, goes beyond suggestion and implication. It is the proof in the pudding. Integrity is the consistent manifestation of trustworthiness, the unwavering alignment of our actions with our words. Integrity is the dependable and consistent enactment of our espoused beliefs, values, and tenets.

Authenticity is about depiction. Integrity is about conviction. Authenticity can be faked. Integrity can't.

Integrity trumps authenticity.

Distrust

Distrust causes us to...

- View others warily, as if they have malicious intent.
- Act in defensive ways in the interest of self-protection.
- Limit our communications.
- Bureaucratize processes/rules/structures that have the effect of constraining others.
- Engage others with skepticism and apprehension.
- Refrain from letting ourselves care.
- Live in a state of disquiet and foreboding.

Distrust tends to restrict our vision, our level of communication, our productivity, our connectedness, and our happiness. Generally, distrust makes us less than we can be and should be. We are better served, both personally and organizationally, when we extend distrust *only* to those who have proven they deserve it.

Trust is by far the better default setting (unless we like living in a world with constant anxiety and suspicion).

(T)Rust

Rust is the oxidation of iron or steel that is manifested in the accumulation of brownish residue on the metal. We've all seen and touched rust. It has the effect of encumbering or inhibiting. It takes the "shine" off of metal. It causes hinges to squeak and eventually freeze up completely. Rust is abrasive and unsightly. Rust implies a disregard for care and attention. Left unaddressed, rust will eventually eat completely through metal, compromising it in all ways.

In organizational work, the lack of trust has the same "oxidizing" effect that rust has on metal. Little by little, day by day, inch by inch, the look and feel and effectiveness of the organization is compromised by that lack of trust. Without the "T," we are left with "rust."

Both in the care and maintenance of metal and in the care of maintenance of organizations, simple attention and a little preventive maintenance are all it takes to keep "rust" at bay. It's really not that hard, and the benefits of that attentive/preventive maintenance are immense.

When trust is absent, "rust" remains.

The Immeasurable Soft Data

In the book titled *Presence* (2005), Peter Senge, et al, state the following: "Not only does overreliance on measurement doom modern society to continuing to see a world of things rather than relationships, it also gives rise to the familiar dichotomy of the 'hard stuff' (what can be measured) versus the 'soft stuff' (what can't be measured). If what's measurable is 'more real', it's easy to relegate the soft stuff, such as the quality of interpersonal relationships and people's sense of purpose in their work, to a secondary status. **This is ironic because the soft stuff is often the hardest to do well and the primary determinant of success or failure."** (p. 192) (Bold text is my embellishment).

But, how do we collect that soft data? We can…

- Actually get to *know* the people in the organization.
- Ask folks what's going well and what's not going well.
- *LISTEN*, when others are speaking.
- NEVER nip people back in public. EVER. (Even when they may need it.)
- Walk the facilities, walk the grounds.
- Talk *personally* to our customers (not through surveys).
- Get trusted others to interface with our organization, then provide feedback to us about their experience(s).
- Make the work environment safe for dissenting voices.

We could probably add more strategies to this list, but it's mostly about creating a trusting, open, and inclusive environment that values transparency and full disclosure. Both are essential qualities for raising the cultural average.

Micromanagers

"Micromanagers" sounds like a dirty word, doesn't it? Few of us that have worked for/with micromanagers have enjoyed the experience.

Micromanagers feel they have to control or be involved in every step of the process. They tend to layer reporting requirements on top of already onerous production challenges. They often perseverate on the wrong metrics, the micro (and less consequential) stuff, mostly because that's the stuff that's easiest to measure. Micromanagers regularly "burn up" way too much time in called meetings or ad hoc conversations in which they're drilling for information/

data that is procurable without pulling the worker bees off task. They believe permission trumps production (thus progress).

What kind of employees do micromanagers lose? Those who prefer to create and innovate in pursuit of a noble cause. They lose talented team players (who usually drift away quietly). They lose those who care about and prefer to pursue the big picture stuff, not the minutiae.

Maybe "micromanager" *is* a dirty word after all.

Caring

Some leaders seem to feel they must put on the armor of "not caring" in order to appear strong. They feel that knowing the troops too well, or having too close relationships with them, somehow compromises their ability to make the hard decisions.

I don't think so. In fact, I believe developing strong and positive relationships with membership throughout the organization is critical to being an effective leader and to shaping a healthier organizational culture. Healthy workplace relationships tend to provide leaders with richer insight into interdependent functions and unique performance. They also affect more honest feedback loops. Better employee effort almost always results when strong relationships are present. As well, leaders gain deeper understanding of skill sets and job "fit" among team members. Finally, stronger organizational culture is a derivative of healthy relationships among and between team members.

Caring almost always begets caring in return. Which of us doesn't need that?

Whine Vaccine

Whining is the act of bellyaching about something (everything?) without investing oneself in the process of making it (whatever it is) better. "Sick" organizations are full of whiners; their toxic behavior seems never to be checked. "Healthy" organizations also have whiners, but the culture of the organization marginalizes them. It's similar to our physical bodies always being host to some dangerous bacteria/viruses; if the body is healthy those dastardly creatures are kept at bay.

So, what do organizations that are "whine vaccinated" look/feel/smell like? Their culture is built around *EVERYONE* owning the problems perceived, and *EVERYONE* being responsible for trying to improve upon them (not just report them). Venting is allowed, but should always be declared as such, and accompanied by possible solutions. Fit organizations constantly build into their thinking an IMPORTANT-VS-URGENT barometer where the important always trumps the urgent (unless safety is involved). These healthy organizations live, breath, and act upon the belief that perfection is not the goal; getting better, everyday, on purpose, *IS*. Finally, healthy organizations systemically notice and acknowledge and celebrate efforts at getting better - no matter how small.

Whiners make sick organizations sicker; healthy organizations make whiners scarcer.

Trust and Attention

Trust and Attention are not the same thing, but they have a symbiotic relationship. Attention can lead to Trust, but more often Trust leads to Attention.

From a leadership perspective, Trust is the precursor to followership. Others *only* follow us (or our ideas/thinking) when they have developed some trust in us. That Trust flows as a direct conclusion on the part of others that we are what we say we are, we do what we say we'll do, we believe what we say we believe, and we act in consistent alignment with our articulations.

Then and only then will others afford us their regular and sustained Attention.

Both Trust and Attention evaporate when we take them for granted, *OR* when we leverage them for inconsequential or self-serving purposes. And they should.

Both Trust and Attention must be viewed and cherished by us as treasures of great value, for that they are. And, they are critical components of organizations with healthy cultures.

Morale Problems

What causes morale problems among the troops? Sometimes, it's uncertainty about the direction (or the nobility of the direction) of the organization. Often, feeling devalued by leadership de-energizes the team. Having a lack of voice in organizational decisions always causes heartburn. An absence of transparency within the organization (usually springing from dismal communications) is a typical trigger for malcontent. Ambiguity about expectations almost always causes organizational angst. Feeling as if one's talents/abilities/skills/knowledge are being wasted is a real downer. Loss of trust between organizational members or between organizational layers is a frequently cited cause of morale problems.

Rarely is low morale about feeling overworked and/or underpaid. These are just less abstract symptoms of the root causes in the list above.

As leaders we should think of every one of those catalysts as a form of "disease" that can infect an organization. Skillful and effective leaders can and do proactively interdict the "infection" likelihood of each. It takes some thought, it takes effort, it takes work, it takes integrity... It also takes intentionally deploying immunization countermeasures for each.

And, the work is never done - attention to the health and wellbeing of the organization (just as with our bodies) is a daily endeavor.

Team Learning

The healthiest organizations are learning organizations. Their culture embodies both a desire and an expectation that learning is fundamental to the organization.

Moving away from "training" and toward a model of *learning* together, often in self-selected directions, is a powerful component of healthy organizations. As well, cross-pollination is a critical ingredient for encouraging innovation. Specialists and technocrats tend to think all other functions of the other organization spoke outward from their "division." Ambidextrous thinkers and workers understand more fully the webbed nature of organizations. Thus, learning across departmental boundaries, across specialty areas, and even beyond the professional genre can energize an organization.

At some point, every organizational member should become a "teacher." Teaching something to others is one of the most powerful ways of pushing knowledge or skill into one's long-term memory. Knowledge is not a thing. Rather, it must be viewed as something that is living, dynamic, emerging, evolving, and malleable. Sharing that knowledge is a powerful tool to both internalize the learning, and to also trigger creativity. It is also a powerful stimulant for raising the cultural average.

Professional Malnourishment

We need nourishment for our professional lives just as our bodies need nourishment. And, just as our physical wellness depends on a variety of healthy nutrients, so does our professional wellbeing depend on our consumption of an array of wholesome inputs.

What might some of those professional nutrients be?

- Watching and learning from masters of our craft.
- Finding and engaging with quality mentors within our field of endeavor.
- Regularly consuming new learning (books, articles, videos, audios) related to our work.
- Networking with a wide variety of practitioners, both within and outside our profession.
- Dabbling with creative and innovative practices, both for the novelty of it and for the potential breakthrough experiences.

- Learning beyond our particular profession from those who are performing in exemplary fashion in some other field, with an eye for transferable practices.

Just as our bodies need the macronutrients of proteins, fats, and carbohydrates so do we need, in our professional lives, the macronutrients of experiences, exposures, and engagement. In both body wellness and professional wellness, we make choices everyday about what we consume. The inputs dictate the outputs.

To choose not to nourish ourselves professionally is to choose to be professionally malnourished. You probably know how that story ends.

Fail!

Failure comes in two different varieties - wholesome and wimpy.

Wimpy failure looks like this:

- Didn't care to start with.
- Didn't try very hard.
- Afraid to go all in.
- Hedged the bets.
- Selfishly framed endeavor.
- Meaningless project to start with.
- Wasted energy, wasted time.

Wholesome failure looks like this:

- Tried hard, missed the goal.
- Invested fully, but no soap.
- Planned well, deployed poorly.
- Lofty goal, just fell a little short.
- Service-oriented.
- Picked the wrong team members.

- All guns blazing, not quite enough bullets.
- Learned a ton from it, even if a bit painful.

One of my friends is fond of saying, "A good loser is still a loser." I don't agree. We *ALL* experience failure. It's just part of life. Failing (or losing) can make us better, or it can lessen us. We get to determine that much from the get-go, which has a whole lot to do with whether we end up failing or not.

By thinking big, by trying hard, by choosing worthy, we get to frame the outcome (whether we reach the goal or not).

Same goes for healthy organizations. The culture of the organization should support this kind of thinking.

Enemies and Diseases

What causes organizations to begin to flounder? Enemies, such as complacency, distraction, mission creep, bureaucratization, and protectionism, interdict organizational success. As well, diseases in the form of overconfidence, too-big-for-your-britches-ness, loss of customer focus, de-energizing processes, and prioritizing profit over quality (whether in products or services) chip away at the health of the organization.

These things act in two ways to bring us down. As enemies, they behave as committed antagonists bent on our demise, sometimes very overtly, sometimes clandestinely. As diseases, they slowly drain our energy, our defenses, our immunities, while we're not even aware of it until it's too late (thus, mitigating our performance).

So what are the remedies for both? Diligence, astuteness, preparedness, fitness, renewal, Renewal, RENEWAL!

(All of those remedies, by the way, are completely within our control. And, all have much to do with self-awareness and self-directed growth).

Raising the Cultural Average

We go crazy when...

- Others "just don't get it."
- We lose touch with reality.
- We don't understand why.
- The tasks and the outcomes don't seem to mesh.
- The effort/thinking/motivations are scattered all over the place.
- Decisions make absolutely no sense.
- Hurting others becomes the norm.
- We can't seem to get all the pieces to "fit."
- The workload seems all askew.
- Complaining trumps complimenting.
- A sense of futility pervades.
- The work is simply undoable.
- The boss is completely disconnected.

Sound like some work places you've seen? Or been a part of? Craziness is both cause and effect of depression (in humans and in organizations).

Now for the million-dollar question: How do *I* contribute to the craziness?

And a second million-dollar question: How can I stop contributing to the craziness?

Turning toward sanity (i.e., *getting better*) starts with me - one word, one act, one step, one thought, one decision at a time. Our personal health and well-being depends on it, as does that of the organizations we serve.

10

Execution: The Art of Getting It Done

"We see, in summary, that every pattern we define must be formulated in the form of a rule which establishes a relationship between a context, a system of forces which arises in that context, and a configuration which allows these forces to resolve themselves in that context."

- CHRISTOPHER ALEXANDER (*TIMELESS WAYS OF BUILDING*, 1979, P. 253)

I learned a powerful lesson about execution from my high school football coach some 40 years ago. My coach taught us that a high-fallootin' and complex game strategy didn't mean a thing if it couldn't be executed (or wasn't executed correctly). He constantly reminded us that even the simplest plans and plays stood a very good chance of success *IF* we would execute them flawlessly. He was a firm believer in the old axiom, "Keep it simple and don't outsmart yourself."

Since those high school football experiences I have seen many complex strategies devised in organizations I've worked in/with. Lots of high-fiving at the announcement of the grand plan, lots of impressive launches, lots of crowing about the sophistication of the strategy, press releases announcing those plans, etc. Then, lots of flops.

Why? Some fizzled for one of the reasons shown below, some for several of those reasons:

- The *need* for the strategy was never communicated well to the team.
- The team was never included in the planning process.
- SPOTS - "strategic plan on top shelf" - The plan was well conceived and developed, placed in a three-ring binder and stored on the top shelf in someone's office.
- Team members never had a clear view of their role in the deployment.
- The articulated outcomes seemed bogus and hollow, fabrications using suspect metrics.
- Leaders of the organization never successfully "embedded" the plan into the daily fabric of the work. "If it's not that important to the bosses, why should it be important to me?" Of course!

With regard to continuous improvement I've come to believe the following (which is why strategic plans are needed in the first place):

1) Plan simply.
2) Plan collectively (everyone gets input).
3) Revisit and revise it constantly (embed it into the daily "talk" and the daily work).
4) Speak often and clearly about the desired outcomes (implied accountability).
5) EXECUTE! Flawlessly, persistently – at least a little, at least everyday (somehow).
6) The "boss" must live it, speak it, notice it, affirm it - with every act and breath.

I am eternally grateful to my coach, for a worthy lesson (about life, and about work).

Successful execution as an organization is dependent on two factors: 1) acting effectively and efficiently in ways that move us toward our goals, and 2) mitigating or minimizing the forces that would inhibit that progress. It's sort of like playing offense and defense at the same time. Obviously, organizational leaders play a critical role in both of those dynamics. As leaders we should constantly be in a mindset of questioning our processes, strategies, protocols, assumptions, premises. And, we should persistently teach and push our team to engage in the same sort of reflective inquiry. What we should not let ourselves (or our teams) do, however, is slip into the unhelpful practice of questioning intent, effort, good will, or commitment. Certainly, there are times when one or more of those are lacking, but the basis of each is "personal" in nature. When we keep our focus, our talk, and our improvement efforts honed in on the "business" rather than "personal" components, a richer and healthier organizational culture persists.

According to Bossidy and Charan (2002), there are seven essential behaviors needed of leaders to optimize execution: 1) Know your people and your business, 2) Insist on realism, 3) Set clear goals and priorities, 4) Follow through, 5) Reward the doers, 6) Expand people's capabilities, and 7) Know yourself.

Understanding some of the common constraints to execution is also important. They are:

- Never enough time (the same dynamic exists for everyone).
- Never enough money (the same dynamic exists for almost everyone).
- The division or team is too large to move nimbly.
- The team becomes a slave to processes.
- There is lack of accountability.
- There is a fundamental failure to connect with the customer.
- Too many layers exist in the organization.
- Messages are garbled.
- The process or project is self-centric rather than customer-centric.

While most systems incentivize the processes (a hallmark of bureaucracy), execution and performance thrive when the system incentivizes the outcomes.

Important to remember is the fact that our goal is not perfection; it must always be improvement. Certainly we'll encounter barriers. However, difficulties and challenges afford opportunities; not the other way around.

There was a time when the "winners" were those who waited for others to innovate, then refined and manufactured and sold the second or third iteration of the innovation. Those are no longer the rules of success. Success belongs to those who push the envelope, take the risk, find and recruit the talent, draw the maps, and create the work conditions for artisans to prosper. Herein lies the domain of execution. Waiting for others to show the way is far more debilitating than it has ever been.

Successful execution is premised on three fundamentals — strong people, strong systems, and positive sources of energy.

PEOPLE

The shortest distance between where our organization is now and where we want it to be is the quality of the people within it. It is the people in our organization that will make it a winner, a loser, or an also ran. While executive leadership is critical, it is and always will be trumped by "local" leadership. The front-line leadership is where execution occurs (or not). Wise organizations invest heavily in the development of the localized leadership.

Not only is substantive and meaningful development essential, empowerment is critical to employee investment and engagement. Involvement and investment are functions of engagement. How best do we get others engaged?

Got Talent?

Wise leaders of organizations understand that the success of the organization is directly proportional to the quality of the people in the organization. The people *ARE* the brand. Thus, attracting, recruiting, hiring, and retaining nothing but top-shelf folks is imperative. Talented folks can work just about wherever they want to (seems like that has been said before).

Some important questions leaders should ask ourselves in relation to the attractiveness of our organization:

1) Why would talent choose our organization over others?
2) Are our vision/mission/goals worthy and noble pursuits, intended to create a better world?
3) Are we being crystal clear about our vision/mission/goals?
4) Are folks in our organization allowed reasonable autonomy in pursuing those goals?
5) Is continuous improvement (personal *and* professional) built into the daily fabric of our work?
6) Are the incentives in our organization built around the success of "we," not "me"?
7) Are our work processes/procedures/protocols fashioned to cater to our best players (not to the average-or-below group)?
8) Is recognizing and noticing good work embedded in the culture of our organization?

How we answer those questions can serve as a useful guide as to what we change and improve in our organizational structures, and what we change and improve in ourselves as leaders.

Great people do great work for great organizations, which, in turn, honor both the great people and their great work.

Trump Card

A great deal has been written about setting objectives and goals, then pursuing them relentlessly. That practice is fundamental to sound execution. Monitoring progress toward those stated objectives is the obvious and next step in that process, to "see how we're doing."

A painfully common phenomenon of this process is that the monitoring takes on a life of its own, and eventually the whole reason for the objectives/goals (call it the *vision*) is lost in the process. We become slaves to the process, rather than to the desired outcomes. When our efforts become focused on the control processes and not on the desired outcomes (the *vision*), we lose our way.

For example, think of the maintenance check-off chart on the inside of the restroom doors of many retail establishments. If we examine these quality-assurance reporting charts, we find that those restrooms are maintained on flawless time schedules. Thus, they must assuredly be persistently clean and sparkling. A quick view at the restroom itself, however, almost always tells a different tale than that reported on the compliance checklist. To be certain, these businesses have formulated a process to ensure the cleanliness of their public restrooms. Yet, the desired outcome often seems NOT to have been realized. The quality of the monitoring is clearly suspect.

The trump card for great organizations is first and foremost to have a committed and passionate team in pursuit of the vision. The data collected around the goals and objectives aligned to that vision should be purely for self-referential purposes, not an outcome in itself.

A company's, a school's, a team's, a family's *brand* is its people, no matter how powerful the systems and processes put in place for quality assurance. Only our people can assure quality, regardless of the product or service we're trying to deliver.

Improv, QBs, and Strategic Plans

Making plans is essential to getting started. We've all heard the old saw about how it's impossible to reach your destination if you don't know where you're going. Of course! We most certainly need to know where we're going and what it is we are trying to accomplish.

The persistent problem with detailed and long-range strategic plans is that they rarely take into account the almost certain eventuality that they will get derailed somehow - by a change in the economy, by missed projections, by the weather, by the departure of key personnel, by _____ (you can fill in the blank).

Two kinds of artisans can inform our practice in this regard:

1) Improvisational comedians are masters at taking the "stem" or the "prompt" (in this discussion, that would be the goal we are trying to achieve), then accepting the environment and stimuli as it comes. They skillfully accept whatever is pitched to them and "blend" that array of variables toward the end in mind. By craft, they discipline themselves to act and respond with a "yes, and..." mentality rather than a "but, we can't/won't/shouldn't..." kind of mindset.

2) Great football quarterbacks are also masters at adaptation. Clearly, the goal for them (almost without exception) is to score. They understand that the called play is nothing more than a starting point, and that there are a myriad of forces bent on derailing that plan. However, those great quarterbacks have not only disciplined themselves to execute the original play, they have also meticulously trained themselves to look for the emerging opportunities when the plan begins to unravel (as it so often does).

A commonality in both of these archetypes is that they have prepared themselves mentally, physically, and emotionally for the possibility of initial failure. And, they have disciplined themselves to consistently turn the initial setbacks/hurdles/opposition to their advantage in the most creative ways. Worth noting also is the fact that the best of both are tenacious and disciplined in preparing themselves to think/speak/act in this adaptive way.

Their adeptness at adaptation is no accident. Making lemonade when presented with nothing but lemons is their modus operandi. Lemonade it is, then! Effective execution depends on it.

Dreamers and Doers

Every team needs both dreamers and doers. Why?

> Dreamers...
> Push boundaries. Help us see what might be.
> Cause us to think about sustainability.
> Assume that risks and failures are part of the process. Challenge us to "get started."
> Shake up the status quo.
> Imagine BIG futures.
> Doers...
> Are goal-oriented.
> Keep us organized.
> Help us stay focused.
> Show us "how" to get it done.
> Take care of the customers. Make and own decisions.
> Tighten the processes.

On rare occasions, one person can be both a Dreamer and a Doer. However, that is not the norm. Every organization needs both types of folks, for wellness and for survival. Organizations that don't have both are already circling the drain.

Starters and Finishers

Some folks are better at starting things and others are better at finishing them.

In construction work, some guys are really skillful at getting the foundation and framework of a building done. They are often not very good at the finish work, like flooring, cabinetry, and painting. Other guys do the finish work. Both skill sets are absolutely essential to producing a quality building. Both kinds of mindsets are required. Neither is more important than the other.

In baseball, some pitchers are great at starting the game, managing batters, throwing pitches that keep the ball "in the park" and base runners tethered to the bases. Other pitchers are great at finishing, throwing 100-mile-per-hour fastballs that one can barely see, much less hit. However, those finishers couldn't (with rare exceptions) do that for seven or eight or nine innings. Both kinds of skills are necessary to win baseball games, and both kinds of mindsets are necessary for success. Neither is more important than the other.

Pick the profession or the endeavor. The same sort of starters-finishers dichotomy exists. To be sure, there are other "roles" and other "role players" that fit somewhere along the continuum between starters and finishers. The point, however, is this: we need each kind of "player" on a successful team. They all bring something unique and important to the task. And, of course, none is more important than any of the others. All have a critical role in executing the plan.

Saboteurs

Damage and destruction occur at the hand of organizational saboteurs. Sometimes that harmful work is done quite intentionally. Other times, however, it is the product of the unwitting.

Tools of Willful Sabotage (via the ill-intentioned):

- Insistence on adherence to the rules/processes - slavery to the letter of the law.
- Pervasive use of committees.
- Talking "it" to death.
- Introducing distractors - taking focus off the vision.
- Incessant wordsmithing.
- Constant rehashing of past decisions.
- Being stuck on the starting line – a reluctance to say "GO!"
- Aversion to ownership.
- Continual permission seeking.

Tools of Unwitting Sabotage (via the well-intentioned):

- Insistence on adherence to the rules/processes - slavery to the letter of the law.
- Pervasive use of committees.
- Talking "it" to death.
- Introducing distractors - taking focus off the vision.
- Incessant wordsmithing.
- Constant rehashing of past decisions.
- Being stuck on the starting line – a reluctance to say "GO!"
- Aversion to ownership.
- Continual permission seeking.

There are some rather obvious similarities, no? Regardless of the motivations, sabotage is sabotage. And saboteurs are saboteurs, irrespective of intentions.

Constantly reflecting on what we're doing, why we're doing it, and how we might do it better can help us avoid the sabotage trap (both of the ill- and the well-intentioned varieties). It's the only way to execute effectively and to improve continuously.

Bobbleheads

Most of us have worked on a team or in an organization that had some bobbleheads. These are the folks that smile, nod, and pretend to agree (whether they do or not). Some classic "symptoms" of bobblehead-itis are:

1) The disinclination to participate fully in crafting solutions.
2) The continual insertion of the question stem of "Yeah, but... " into almost all discussions.
3) The unwillingness to energetically engage in the deployment of an agreed upon strategy.
4) Hiding from, or the outright fear of, responsibility.

Organizational leaders can, by the environments we create, encourage or discourage the number and impact of the bobbleheads. How? By ensuring full and open disclosure of information relevant to the organization. We can also make sure *all* members of the team/organization have voice. We should NEVER punish members for using the voice we have given them. The environment must be made safe for dissent. Leaders should praise the team for the "wins," and own the "losses" personally. Finally, we must constantly review, revisit, and revise (i.e., continuous improvement mode).

The more complex the problems we face, the more unclear the "right" solutions will be. All voices need to be heard, all minds are needed in the crafting of solutions. In order to execute with fidelity, all shoulders are needed at the wheel.

The Don't-Quote-Me Gang

One frequently noted workplace frustration is working for/with folks in leadership positions who seem unwilling to "own" or put their decisions in print. It is extremely frustrating to not be able to get a straight answer from those leaders, even if the answer is simply (and often most appropriately), "It's your call."

Leaders who operate in that don't-quote-me type of mentality seem to want it both ways – the title and the money that goes with leadership roles, but none of the accountability that accompanies those roles. Faux leaders seek to dodge bullets, to stay below the radar, and to live a Teflon-like existence. That same mindset also gains for them the general disdain of those who find themselves down the chain of command. Their subordinates constantly feel as if they are walking on a tightrope, with no safety net or support from the boss. Those willing to step up and make tough decisions often get bloodied up (while the boss is conveniently well-distanced from the catastrophe and/or the accountability).

This sort of don't-quote-me leadership tends to foster a state of inertia in the organization. Team members who don't feel empowered and supported frequently exhibit very little in the way of boldness and risk-taking in the interest of pushing organizational objectives.

Having witnessed this dynamic time and again, I determined NOT to treat the folks with whom I work in similar fashion. A far better approach, I think, is to give them autonomy, give them authority, invest in their development, and coach them in the ways of right thinking and service orientation. As one of my mentors says, "If they act within policy and law, support their decisions. If you don't like their decisions, discuss it privately with them and coach them up. But never publicly cut their legs out from under them."

You can quote me on this.

Mess Cleaners

My wife once asked one of her 2nd graders what kind of work her dad did for a living. The youngster replied that her dad was a janitor. The little girl said that whenever she asked her dad what he did at work, the answer was always the same: "Baby, I clean up messes all day."

In fact, the girl's dad did spend a great deal of his time cleaning up messes, just not the kinds of messes janitors and custodians deal with. Her dad, it turns out, was an executive at a multi-national company.

Leadership always entails a healthy dose of mess cleaning.

Messes get made when:

- Important messages get miscommunicated or misinterpreted.
- The processes/protocols of an organization get misaligned with its mission and/or vision.
- Incentives end up rewarding the least productive or those who game the system.
- Workplaces become toxic.
- Sacrifices to quality are made in the interest of efficiency.
- Self-preservation trumps collective endeavor.
- Motives become divorced from the goals of the organization.
- People are involved.

Leaders who are diligent and consistent (even persistent) about messaging, about building and sustaining positive relationships, about recognizing and honoring effort as well as achievement, about insisting on authenticity and integrity (and model the same), still have to spend time cleaning up messes.

But leaders who fail in those critical leadership manifestations spend a lot *more* time cleaning up messes, and deal with much larger doses of poor execution.

SYSTEMS
Systems are at play in any organizational endeavor. Only when systems are well considered and outcome-focused do they affect fluid and purposeful execution. The primary assumption regarding execution is that we actually know what we want to accomplish. There's no way to measure that which we can't (or don't) conceive.

Data collection and analysis is critical in the role of effective execution. There are several kinds of data: 1) the "numbers," 2) that which we hear, and 3) that which we observe. Scharmer (2009) suggests a fourth source – 4) data we *feel*. Indeed. Counter-intuitively, that which is most important is often invisible to the eye as well as being invisible to our metrics.

Wise leaders are attuned to all four data sources. What we decide to measure and score has a funny way of becoming important to the team. Therefore, it is imperative for purposes of execution that we create effective scoring metrics for what we value. If the collection and analysis of data is not used intentionally to affect improvement, then the process portends a significant waste of resources. Narrowing our primary objectives is critical for effective execution; focusing on everything means focusing on nothing. We should be committed to using data, while at the same time being skeptical of that very data. We should analyze it, discuss it, dissect it, and, if necessary, be prepared to dismiss it.

As we map and deploy execution strategies, it is important to avoid becoming slaves to the processes we contrive. We ought to take care to focus on outcomes, not processes. We should also be perfectly willing to stop doing things that are not substantively contributing to our execution strategies. After Action Reviews (AARs), in some form, should always be a part of our processes. Charging from one project into the next without reflection and assessment provides nothing in the way of learning for our organizations.

Eye on the Ball

One of the real challenges in life and in leadership is learning to "keep your eye on the ball." Whether it's baseball, golf, football, or tennis, the masters of the game learn early on to center their attention on the ball, for those precious moments of time at which the ball is in play.

It sounds easy, but there are a gazillion distractions that vie for the attention of the athlete at those moments - the weather, the crowd, the noise, the opponent's chatter, the movement of the opponent, the desire to "peek" ahead to see the outcome, etc.

Just like in life. Just like in leadership. Tons of distractions vie for our attention, some purely happenstance and circumstantial, some purposeful attempts to cause our failure. And, just like the master athlete, we must discipline ourselves through persistent practice to stay focused on what matters most. Why? Because missing the ball does not advance our cause.

Winning - in sports, in life, in leadership - is the direct result of our ability to "keep our eye on the ball."

Distractions

Distractions divert our attention, they suck our energy, they waste our time, and they create disharmony. They can spring from external events/people, from poorly structured environments, from weak or devious team members, or misaligned metrics and incentives.

A fundamental job of leaders (whether they be moms, teachers, coaches, or bosses) is to minimize and/or eliminate distractions.

How? By relentlessly attending to...

- Vision, mission, goals, objectives (too many of these are a distraction in itself).
- Praising and supporting acts aligned to those guiding elements.
- Noticing and candidly calling out acts that don't align to those guiding elements.
- Permanently removing persistent distractors.

That can't and won't happen if the leaders are sissies, unfocused, unclear, or ... distracted.

Forward View

Continuous improvement is a process by which we stay focused on the future, with only intermittent and brief backward looks. Effort, energy and attention are primarily focused on the future, on getting better, everyday, somehow, on purpose.

It's a little like driving a car and keeping most of our attention on what's in front of us. Of course, we take backward looks (via mirrors, please) to briefly and intermittently see what is behind us that might inform our next steps. But, the broad view through the windshield is where attention is rightly focused. That view helps us determine speed, direction, evasive action, acceleration, braking, course alteration, etc.

In the case of continuous improvement the brief backward looks are represented by data analysis, by after action reports, by rituals and celebrations. None of those should take huge amounts of time - just enough to inform our next steps. We must keep our attention primarily on the road ahead. Attending to the forward view is fundamental to effective execution.

It helps also to know where it is we want to go. Skillful leaders help us envision those destinations.

Agile

Agility is critical for those who lead organizations. Agility is just as critical for the organizations they lead.

Some critical indicators of agility:

- Heightened awareness - a keen sense of what's going on around us and of healthy response options to those conditions.
- Nimble responsiveness - the ability to jump, seize, dodge, charge, change direction, deflect, react to situational/contextual stimuli with quick suppleness.

- Flexibility - the physical and structural underpinnings of nimbleness; the willingness and ability to stretch our thinking, our responses, our inclusiveness, our protocols, our schedules (but never our principles).

Know any organizations like this? Know any leaders like this?

Being *stuck*, on the other hand, is a clear symptom of lack of agility. Know any organizations like this? Know any leaders like this?

Profit, or Value?
What we measure tends to drive our behavior.

If we're in business purely to make profit, then reducing costs, cutting waste, limiting employee benefits, constantly negotiating down our supply chain vendors, will all improve the bottom line. Profit becomes our master in this case, because that is the measurement we have chosen to define our "success."

Value, on the other hand, is a very different standard.

Value is created

by crafting self-actualizing work (both in ourselves and for our employees),

by engaging in meaningful (not just profitable) acts,

by investing in acts of integrity,

by putting service before profit,

by contributing to the community/society,

by thinking in terms of relationship-building rather than transactional exchanges.

We can make money (and a living) either way.

Life is better when we focus on adding value.

Death March

One of the prominent features of bureaucratic inertia and dysfunction is the slow, painful, excruciating process of having meetings that are not well-conceived, conducted without focus, and/or are ambiguous in purpose. "Death by meeting" has become a fairly common phrase heard around the water cooler in organizations of all shapes and sizes.

As an organizational leader of many years I am guilty as the next "chair" of presiding over painful, non-fruitful, excruciating meetings. Managing meetings well is tricky business, but we can do this. Effective execution depends on it.

We can do better by crafting and managing meetings with these strategic features:

- Start and stop on time.
- Clearly indicate decisions to be made.
- Allow all players to participate, but not bird walk.
- Make agendas available to all ahead of the meeting.
- Keep agendas tight, and relevant to the work at hand.
- Be clear and specific about action steps and follow-up benchmarks.
- Require opinion givers to defend/support their position in relation to the objectives.
- Honor all informed opinions/contributions (but quickly curtail the uninformed or unprepared ones).

Huddles, Not Meetings

According to Peter Drucker, "...one either meets or works. One cannot do both at the same time." Oh how we punish ourselves with meetings!

I have heard it proposed that meetings should be conducted more like huddles on a football field. The analogy makes sense when you consider these similarities:

- Everyone shows up with *ONLY* the needed equipment (you never see a smartphone or laptop or briefcase or lunchbox in a football huddle).
- The purpose of the gathering has been in development and pervasively-communicated for at least the week prior.
- The "agenda items" are all action items, not discussion items.
- Everyone at the meeting is clear about their roles and the absolute necessity of their successful deployment.
- They're brief, *really* brief. Start and stop times are perfectly clear and religiously adhered to (tardiness and chit-chat are not allowed).
- The invitees are few, and all have direct relevance to the gathering.
- All the attendees understand the common technical language being used (no wasted time explaining stuff that is assumed to be known and understood).
- Everyone stands (no sitting allowed).
- The subsequent performance outcomes are clear to the *WORLD* (the ultimate in transparency - real and tangible accountability).
- The persistent "failers" get un-invited pretty quickly.

Wouldn't it be nice to see more meetings run like a football huddle?

Hole Shooting

One of the biggest challenges an organizational leader faces is to get teams to craft and deploy quality strategies for moving forward.

In my early years of leadership I would make the mistake of simply floating an open question to the group, fishing for ideas on how best to proceed (on whatever topic was moot at the time). Again and again I experienced questioning looks, shrugs, acquiescent responses, and even bland questions meant to dodge the issue. I would often get frustrated at this dynamic, wanting to blame team members for being disengaged, for lacking motivation to tackle our organizational problems, or for simply trying to fly below the radar (in the interest of self-preservation).

While some of that stuff may have, in fact, been at play, I came to understand that the condition of stasis was more *my* problem (as the leader) than theirs. The reality is that most of us, regardless of our job title or organizational role, stay focused on the contexts and circumstances that are most relevant to our particular assignment. Few spend time thinking about the big picture challenges to an organization because, frankly, they are swamped with the flood of smaller picture stuff that rolls in each day.

Far too belatedly, I came around to a better approach to having team conversations about big picture strategy, forecasting, and organizational response efforts. I learned to leverage my own obsessiveness in thinking about the sticky stuff we deal with in organizations, those things that wake me up at 2:00 a.m. with my mind whirring away. I began using a process I'll call "hole shooting" to help get the best thinking and fuller engagement of the leadership team. It goes something like this: I would try to think of a few (two at least) alternative approaches to the situational challenge with which we were faced. I would put those options on the table and *invite* team members to "shoot holes in 'em." This approach seems to garner much higher levels of engagement from team members. Oddly, the human mind seems more adept at finding fault than finding worthiness.

So be it. At least we could get off dead center using this method of strategy deconstruction. In a backward sort of way, we could tease out the least vulnerable strategies. Good enough, so long as it provided impetus for moving our organization in the direction we needed it to go. It represented yet another way to improve our execution.

Imperfect Solutions

Imperfect solutions are really the only kind of solutions that exist.

Even if we have found/crafted a solution that just seems "perfect" - for this time or this situation - circumstances change, people act or react or balk, technology changes, the world evolves. Something or someone compromises the solution. Sooner or later, those seemingly perfect solutions prove less.

When we assume that all solutions are imperfect we intuitively default to keeping our finger on the pulse of said solutions. Thus, we are always looking for ways to improve them, revise them, rebuild them, or, revamp them completely.

Then, we can come up with a brand new set of imperfect solutions. That's the way continuous improvement works.

Walkabout

There is an old adage about taking care of the land: "The best fertilizer for the fields is the footprints of the owner." My wife and I have learned the truth of this proverb firsthand, on our ranch. Nothing we do for/with our property is as valuable as actually "walking" it regularly. Through that process we get a sense of its rhythms, its pulse, its strengths, its needs. Scharmer (2009) speaks of his farmer father taking the family on Sunday walks across their land. He describes the informative power of actually walking about the land that one relies on for sustenance and livelihood.

What happens in our workplace if we actually "walk the land," or stroll through our business, or make a site visit to a branch store, or converse with our customers in the reception area? Here are some of the outcomes I believe we realize:

- We will see both desired crops (which we planted) and the weeds (which we didn't).

- Areas of need will be exposed - fences in disrepair, wash outs, fallen trees, dead animal carcasses, depleted plots of land, etc.
- We will likely step in some kind (or several kinds) of poop. When we do, we must remember that poop is a remarkable fertilizer.
- The diversity and circularity of life will confront us on many levels. We must remember that these things are essential for its richness.

To be sure, it is much easier to stay in the cabin, by the fire; or in the office, doing paperwork. However, regular walkabouts are excellent "nutrition" for both the organization and its members.

Attractors

Learning must be an embedded part of the work of well-executing organizations. Leaders should strive to build and embed both personal and professional development into the culture of the organization.

The healthiest organizations are the ones in which the members have relatively equal access to resources, "nutrients," and opportunities while at the same time understanding and subscribing (voluntarily) to the overriding vision and its subsequent missions. Leaders are the ones that cobble and hone the conditions for this sort of entrepreneurial environment to exist. They paint the picture and leverage resources. They cheer and support the members in their bilateral pursuit of both individual and organizational success. Flat organizations, as opposed to those that are highly layered and hierarchically structured, contribute to this schema in the most self-actualizing way(s). That necessarily means autonomy for the divisions, mastery of the skills/knowledge within each, and commitment to the overarching purpose.

Such organizations tend to be attractors of talent. "News" of these kinds of organizations travels – via pool talk, via social media, via informal networks. By and large, organizations get the employees they deserve. If we don't have very intentional processes for the recruitment and development of talented artisans we will get vendors. The choice is ours.

Dissent

Dissent is an interesting word. It is easily recognizable as a position of disagreement. However, it does not generally imply the same kinds of negative connotations as words like argument or dispute. Dissent seems more aligned with concepts such as disagreement, debate, or expressed differences of opinion. Dissent suggests pushback via more respectful manifestations than, say, protests or resistance.

Dissent is a powerful nutrient for healthy organizations. It serves as a marker to indicate fundamental opposition to an idea or proposal or practice within the organization. On the surface, dissent seems disruptive. It has the effect of slowing down the conversation (or directives). Dissent feels inconvenient.

However, dissent also has the effect of helping us clarify positions and interests. It helps us get a better view of the long-term prospects of a proposal or idea. Dissent also helps us gain a better view of the motivations of those involved in the dialogues, both the proponents and the dissenters. In either case, those motivations can be authentic and righteous, or they can be quite egocentric. Oddly, dissent seems more readily available as a tool, yet less used, in organizations where leaders foster high levels of transparency and full disclosure. That seems almost paradoxical.

Wise leaders should go out of their way to ensure an organizational culture that is safe for dissent. Dissent most certainly indicates opposition of some sort. Those wise leaders know, however, that opposition that is squelched or punished or harassed or demeaned or disparaged or impugned expresses itself in much uglier ways than simple *dissent*.

Continuous Improvement

Fundamentally, healthy organizations are about *life* – growth, development, succession. Regardless of their purpose for existence, organizations must attend to that life cycle (unless, of course, they were envisioned and created for the sole purpose of being sold).

Thus, a mindset of continuous improvement must be intertwined into the fabric of the organization. To be sure, we can find and purchase any of hundreds of continuous improvement "packages" or models. It doesn't, however, have to be that difficult, and it certainly doesn't have to be expensive. Just like integrity, right thinking, and ethical behavior, continuous improvement is the manifestation of a belief system, not the result of a ritual. Continuous improvement should be self-sustaining and generative, not forced and contrived.

Some simple questions that drive a continuous improvement mindset are: What are we doing? Why are we doing it? How is what we are doing aligned with our vision? What are we not doing that we ought? How can we do better that which needs doing? When leaders make these questions, and those like them, part of the daily, weekly, monthly conversations with members throughout the organization, the habit of thinking in terms of continuous improvement begins to meld its way into the actions and thinking of the organization.

If reflections upon those questions expose misguided effort, misguided worthiness, or misguided energy, then it's time for us to learn and grow a little (or *change* something).

Getting better, every day, on purpose... It's a sure path to effective execution.

Better

Not perfect. Just *better*. That is the message of continuous improvement.

If we can condition ourselves into viewing learning, growth, improvement as a *PROCESS*, rather than a destination, we begin to understand that imperfection is the constant reality.

We need not wait for perfection to try the next strategy, to launch the next project, to engage in the next initiative, to experiment with the next software package, to pilot a new approach toward engagement with customers.

Pessimists insist on perfect solutions before proceeding; that's one way they validate the (perceived) bleakness of their current circumstances.

Optimists take the chance, step across the threshold, hit the "start" button, all with the belief that rounding the first corner, and each subsequent one, will provide new learning that will put them that much closer to....BETTER.

Effective and/or Efficient?

I once worked in an organization that espoused as one of its primary goals the deployment of "effective *and* efficient" operations. I loved it! We clearly articulated for the world our intent to conduct business using only the best practices known to man, and to do it all in the most cost efficient manner. Who could argue with that?

I have since learned that effective and efficient sometimes don't dovetail so nicely. How should we respond when an "or" seems to supplant the "and" as the conjunction in that "effective and efficient" phrase?

When effectiveness and efficiency seem to knock heads with each other instead of playing nicely together, our default position *must* fall to the effectiveness side of that ledger.

Here's why. Slavery to efficiency models has the effect of diminishing the human element (the relationship management processes) in organizations. Effectiveness almost always entails activating the very best that humans have to offer, which rarely happens without huge investments in the nurturing and development of relationships. Those things take time and effort, which runs contrary to the purist notion of efficiency models.

Effective should always trump efficient (if they can't play nicely together, that is).

Tolerance Limits

Not everyone agrees with my belief that folks work best when they have autonomy over their work patterns and environment. Some wonder if there is a limit to my tolerance in that regard. Indeed, there is.

When we share a common vision of a better future and when we have clear goals that we're pursuing with that future in mind, it is similar to climbing a mountain to reach its peak. There are many paths that can be taken, and many rates of progress that can be utilized while climbing those paths (dependent on contextual factors). I believe people work best and are most productive when given significant latitude in their choice of paths and tempo that best moves them/us toward the espoused goal(s).

Our tolerance levels should hit their limit when team members take a path headed down the mountain instead of up (e.g., quit pursuing the team goals or start chasing erroneous ones) and/or are moving at a pace that is unacceptably slow. In either of those cases, intervention is required, usually in the form of redirection or separation.

Here is recipe that works for effective execution:

Clarity of purpose + Focused effort + Constant progress = Achievement

Mistaken

Some of us work in organizations in which it is not safe to make mistakes. It's not that mistakes are not made, they're just hidden, often in very ingenious ways. These are the organizations that foster distrust, that feel tense, that inhibit the free flow of communication, that squelch transparency. They're also the organizations that serve their customers, both the internal ones and the external ones, abysmally. These are dying organizations (though they often don't know it yet).

Quality organizations make it safe to make mistakes (as long as it's not the same mistake repeated again and again). Mistakes are understood to be the natural derivative of effort, of pushing boundaries, of trying something beyond what is "required." These organizations feel collegial. They foster collaboration. They invite the sharing of lessons learned. They inculcate full disclosure and engender trust. And, they tend to freely own their mistakes and make them right. These high-functioning organizations also happen to be the ones with the most energized employees (internal customers) and satisfied external customers.

I've worked in both kinds. Life is simply too short to spend it working in dysfunctional organizations.

SOURCES OF ENERGY

Amazing performance DOES NOT spring from the pages of a personnel handbook or procedures manual. Powerful performance, driven by effective execution, originates in quality people. Quality team players cannot, and should not, be thought of as automatons. Rather, they must be viewed as independent contractors and artisans. Pink (2012) rightly notes that quality players function best in environments in which they have autonomy over their work, the freedom to exercise mastery within the contexts of their unique talents, and when pursuing goals of worthy purpose.

Choosing the right people matters a great deal. Strategies are carried out best, by the best. Thus, we are wise to recruit well. Buckingham and Coffman (1999) assert that leaders should spend the most time with their best people, as it is the only way to remain focused on excellence. Consequently, wise leaders build processes and procedures around the strongest players, not the weakest.

As leaders we must ask if our procedures, regulations, and processes encourage innovation and risk-taking, or stifle it. If the latter is the case, then the question begs: Who prospers in our organization? The bold, innovative, and talented? Or, the compliant, fearful, and tepid?

According to S. M. R. Covey (2006) there are 13 behaviors in which leaders should partake which enhance organizational trust and spawn effective execution. Those behaviors are: straight talk, demonstrate respect, create transparency, right wrongs, show loyalty, deliver results, get better, confront reality, clarify expectations, practice accountability, listen first, keep commitments, and extend trust.

Block (2008) posits, "To be more specific, leaders are held to three tasks: to shift the context within which people gather, name the debate through powerful questions, and listen rather than advocate, defend, or provide answers." (p. 73). These authors allude to the power of relationships as the underlying force for effective execution.

Having a simple but tight alignment for the work is critical. Is the need for the product/service we are providing crystal clear to the organizational membership? Is it embedded and articulated in a way that every member of the organization knows his/her role in making it happen? Are there simple, understandable metrics by which we can assess and discuss our success and efforts at improvement?

To many, leading implies orchestrating, directing, driving. In fact, leading is more about influence, about nuance, about persuasion. Management is about moving stuff – stuff like inventory, information, schedules, data, cargo, etc. Leadership, on the other hand, is about moving people. It is the art of helping folks to do something they wouldn't have done on their own, or stimulating them to do something at a quicker pace than they would have accomplished on their own. The most effective leaders accomplish both managing and leading, simultaneously. The skills sets for managing and leading are a bit different, so some leaders find that they have to compensate for deficiencies in one or the other by working through/with others on the team to accomplish important and necessary managing or leading tasks for which they, themselves, are not particularly well-equipped. This self-knowledge, with subsequent adaptability, has everything to do with the quality of execution that occurs.

NegAttrition

Attrition is the slow bleeding down of someone or some entity. It's the proverbial "death by a thousand duck nibbles." Not only does attrition diminish effectiveness and strength, it does it in a protracted way. Attrition is the gradual sucking of life and vitality from a person or an organization. The downward pressure is relentless.

Negativity is the foot soldier of attrition. Positivity is the combatant of attrition.

The good news is we can choose how we think, we can choose what we read, we can choose what we listen to, and we can choose who we associate with. As leaders we can also influence organizational norms in similar ways.

Attrition is reversible. It's all about the inputs (which, of course, we get to choose).

The Simplest Incentive
Of all the things we have at our disposal to provide incentive for effort, hard work, honesty, achievement, etc., one stands out as the simplest (and least expensive). That one powerful yet simple incentivizer is the word "Thanks."

Interestingly, it seems so hard for many of us to use that word. It's not like its effects diminish with use. Thus, there is really no risk in overuse.

ALL of us love to hear that word spoken in our direction, regardless of whether it was truly deserved, or whether the trigger for its receipt was a menial or insignificant act on our part.

Follow Through
"Follow through" is the experience of the sweet feel of full connection that occurs when we shoot a basketball and just know it's flying true, or when we strike a softball and feel it jump off the bat, or when we stroke a golf ball and know that we've hit "the sweet spot."

In those instances, it is the dynamic of follow through that causes that sensation of rightness. It's as if the initiation of the process naturally and easily flows to its intended completion. Oddly, in those instances, the sensation is one of full connection without the feel of overexertion. It's as if the process simply flows under its own power.

We experience that self-actualizing feel of follow through when intellect, emotion, concentration, and physical effort converge holistically toward the desired outcome. Follow through is the manifestation of truly being "in the zone." Csikszentmihalyi (1997) describes this as "flow."

Follow through can also be experienced in a lot of non-athletic kinds of endeavors. When we successfully blend our intention and effort in order to *complete* the process, we can experience that euphoric feel when doing things like starting a business, fostering a relationship, teaching a lesson, bringing life to a nascent idea, or performing a piece of music.

A couple of conditions are necessary antecedents to experiencing the heavenly sensation of follow through:

1) We've gotta show up. Follow through cannot be done vicariously; it's a first-person event.
2) Follow through is accomplished best and most often when we have purposefully practiced that convergence of intention and effort hundreds (if not thousands?) of times. Consistent follow through is the result of disciplined practice.

Oh, how sweet the feel. It is, in fact, the feel of successful execution.

11

Contextual Astuteness: Navigating the Political Landscape

"We know from science that nothing in the universe exists as an isolated or independent entity."

- Margaret J. Wheatley

One of my mentors is fond of reminding me that, when it comes to dealing with the organizational politics of leadership, we can play the game without "kissing the ring." In order to both play the game and avoid kissing the ring, we must first hone our senses to the myriad variables that make up the contextual landscape. Understanding who the key players are, which groups wield influence, what the non-negotiables are, the norms that govern interactions, and the pressure points are all critical to our ability to lead effectively.

As leaders, we are in the business of engaging with and influencing people. With that constant connection comes the emotional and psychological influence we can potentially bring to bear upon each and every one of the folks we encounter. To add to the complexity, people always and naturally form themselves into groups, subgroups, and splinter groups, each of which have their own motivations, agendas, and foibles. We are, after all, social beings.

Every family, community, nation, culture, team, and subculture has leaders. For leaders to effectively lead, we absolutely must have a well-trained and keen eye for the myriad and shifting political alliances that occur between the individuals and groups over which we presume to assert some sort of influence.

Understanding the context is one thing, mastering it is something else altogether. In gaining that understanding of context we have to practice "looking" – looking inward, looking outward, and looking over, the horizon. Yet, *looking* is not enough. Adeptly navigating within the contexts is the true hallmark of success in leadership.

Connection

Emotion is at the heart of leading (and moving) people. Emotion is driven by things personal. Thus, wise leaders know the power of listening to and remembering the "stories" others share. They learn *about* others, not in a self-serving way, but rather, in order to establish a basis for a trusting relationship. Authentic engagement with others can only be accomplished by getting into their presence, and having personal conversations with them. Getting to know the key players and beginning to understand their sources of power is an important first step in navigating the political landscape (Morgan, 1988).

Critical to navigating successfully in the political landscape is an understanding of the dynamic of resistance. In almost any setting of human interaction in which important decisions are made and actions taken, there exists resistance of one kind or another. As leaders, we must be prepared to encounter resistance on a daily basis, especially if we are being bold about pursuing a worthy and collaboratively crafted organizational vision. Sometimes, the resistors manifest their recalcitrance through rage. With others, resistance may be manifested in more passive, or even subversive, ways. Astute leaders understand that we must understand the resistors if we have hope of either overcoming or mitigating their objections. And they also are cognizant of the fact that resistance often gains traction through political alliances.

Navigating adeptly in political waters is no job for sissies. Neither is it work for those who would prefer to play like such contexts don't exist. Lacking contextual astuteness is similar to a fly that repeatedly flies into and bounces off of a window, despite the fact that it has thousands of eyes. Though it has many eyes, it still does not "see" the barriers that prevent it from accomplishing its goal. As leaders, we simply must learn to "see" the whole and the parts and their connections, all at once.

Spear Dodging

One of the most challenging aspects of leadership is inviting and dissecting feedback. Many leaders abhor (even avoid) the act of inviting feedback from internal/external customers, to their own demise. Collecting what Peter Senge (1990) calls the "soft data" is critical, and it occurs most often through person-to-person feedback loops.

Leaders who choose to seek feedback by actually venturing out of the office or extracting themselves from behind a computer screen will most assuredly receive it. *How* we receive it is critical to the success of our organization. When we invite feedback we should be prepared to hear more bad than good. That is the natural order of things. We should listen carefully to both. Typically, customer engagement and feedback occurs at the extremes of the "happiness" continuum. Folks who are raving fans and folks who are extremely angry are the ones that will make the most

noise. Understand that going in. Strategic care should be taken to hear the voices between those extremes as well.

Engaging in the feedback loop is not and should not be only about hearing the good and bad in relation to our work. Face-to-face or person-to-person engagement is as much about building or repairing or bolstering relationships as it is about hearing praise and/or complaints.

Folks that are heard, really heard, generally are much more willing to join our team or remain on our team or market on behalf of our team. The ones that feel unheard will sharpen up the spears and begin heaving them our way, with amazing relentlessness and accuracy.

We can spend all our time dodging spears, or we can begin a conversation with the spear throwers. Either way, they're gonna get our attention.

The Web, The Network

Beware of any attempt to explain the world in simple terms. What we know from the history of the sciences is that our current understanding is rarely completely correct, and often it is drastically astray. Linkages between humans and between organizations are numerous. They are at once conceptual, physical, intellectual, and spiritual in nature. Our intertwined relationships are like a river in constant movement – bumping, swirling, upstreaming, stagnating, flooding, trickling, being fed, feeding, lifting, depositing, and containing solids/liquids/gases/plants/animals/minerals. Even our intelligence cannot be thought of in singular terms, as it is a collective construct.

In the midst of trying to make sense of this massive web of interconnectedness, we must understand fully that we are all followers and all leaders. One does not exist without the other. Consequently, knowing and understanding both contexts and origins is critical. And there are always programs that are "running in the background" – just as with our own physical regulation processes of heart rate, temperature, threat monitoring, etc. Organizations have the same type systems running in the background, too.

Bolman and Deal (2006) state, "Organizations and societies are networks as well as hierarchies, and the power of relationships is a crucial complement to the power of position. In simplest terms, network power amounts to the power of your friends minus the power of your enemies." (p. 85) As a result, we can never accomplish our organizational goals alone. We really can't even accomplish organizational goals purely within our organization's network. Understanding and nurturing the network within and without is a prerequisite for success. Networking is best done *before* we need the network.

Pinging valued others should be a part of our daily regimen. In the current milieu of social networks and electronic connectivity, it is easy to "touch base" with others via e-mail, texting, Facebook, etc., just to let them know we are thinking of them. Thinking of them makes them think of us. This tightens the network connections for those moments when we *really* need that other person's help or thinking.

Interconnected

For those who choose the demanding but rewarding path of servant leadership, one of the most challenging tasks we face is to understand the concept of interconnectedness. Highly effective and influential leaders demonstrate the ability to see, and to operate in, both the macro and the micro, simultaneously. This mastery is usually manifested in direct proportion to their understanding of the complex web of interdependency and interconnectedness of the myriad structures, processes, and people that compose the working parts of the organizations they lead.

Organizations resemble greatly the wholeness of a tree, which possesses as much mass below the ground as above. The natural tendency is to think of a tree simply – as a noun, made up of nouns, such as the trunk, branches, leaves, and roots. In reality, however, a tree is a verb, a complex set of structures, processes, and elements (both living and non-living) that are enmeshed in a dynamic, beautiful, and magical dance. When all the leaves, the branches, the trunk, the xylem, the phloem, the minerals, the photosynthesis, the water, the fungal net, the microbial communities – this list goes on and on – are in sync, the result is a beautiful and self-sustaining organism, with each "player" performing its role in perfect harmony.

Organizations should be thought of in the same light. Rich, healthy, and vibrant organizations are the product of that same kind of interconnected harmony that exists in a healthy tree. As servant-leaders, we are charged with the caretaking and wellness of the organization. Consequently, a deep understanding of the structures, the processes, and the elements is critical. As important as understanding the "parts" of the organization is the need to understand the symbiotic *relationships* between and among those parts.

In viewing organizations in this way, we can see patterns and coherent webs as they emerge, extend, and grow. What we don't see is the kind of hierarchical, linear, and contrived structures we do in organizational charts and chains of command. To be strong servant-leaders we must see, and attend to, the whole and the parts, concurrently. And, we must become relationship experts as part and parcel of our work.

We cannot understand a tree through the lens of only one academic discipline. To understand trees deeply we must understand dendrology, ecology, hydrology, biology, biochemistry, entomology, geology, pedology, and a host of other –ologies. Likewise, to be the most effective servant-leaders, we must be on a constant path of personal and professional learning across a broad range of disciplines in order to better understand the very organizations whose health and wellbeing we have been entrusted.

Wholesome Politics

We must understand the political context, the power structures, the influence peddlers, who the good/bad guys are, and how to garner what we need (whether it be resources, support, allies, etc.). What we do *NOT* have to do, in fact should not do, is suspend our principles in order to effectively function in organizational life.

Several strategies can assist us in this pursuit:

- KNOW what we believe.
- Be transparent about our beliefs.
- Resist being openly judgmental/critical of others.
- SAY what we believe, the same way, in many settings.
- ACT in accordance to what we believe (there's that *integrity* thing).
- Avoid pettiness like the plague.
- Always work to raise others up, never to tear them down.

Following this guidance can help us navigate the treacherous waters of organizational politics, with more positive outcomes than negative. Of course, there will be a few "losses" along the way, but engaging in the political milieu in accordance with this advice will at least help us deal with those "losses" without the added burden of a guilty conscience.

Toughness

Those in leadership roles (e.g., parents, managers, owners, captains, teachers, bosses, etc.) must possess a healthy dose of toughness. Not meanness, toughness. Not brutishness, toughness. Not insensitivity, toughness. Not harshness, toughness.

What can toughness look like? Here are some examples:

- Saying "no" when you'd prefer to say "yes" (and vice versa).
- Shouldering the blame to protect valued others and their good work.
- Ignoring a rule/law/protocol and being willing to defend that act.
- Insisting that *people* come before structure(s), foibles and all.
- Sticking to principle even if it means losing friends, employees, jobs.
- Listening attentively even when it's hard to hear merit in the talk.
- Letting right-minded others make some (non-fatal) mistakes, even if you know a "better" way.
- Forgiving, even when it's the last thing you want to do.

Leadership is no job for sissies or the wobbly. Only the tough need apply.

Quitting

I'm no quitter.

However, I have told every employer in my professional career the same thing: "If you get tired of me, if you decide I'm not being effective, if I'm not performing like you want, or if you simply feel the need to 'go a different direction,' just let me know. There's no need to freeze me out, squeeze me out, document me out, or fire me. I'll walk away, without causing a storm."

I use the same kind of thinking with regard to my relationship with an organization and/or its leadership. When we continue to stay in a role in which we are not being effective, or in an organization we are not able to serve well, or continue serving a leader who does not have our confidence, it is impossible for us to function at our fullest capabilities.

Certainly, we can stay with an organization/boss if we believe we can influence the organization's direction or the leader's thinking toward ways to which we can fully subscribe. But, that "staying" should only be done in a way that is not subversive, divisive, or insubordinate. If we can't "stay" with integrity and good will and fully invested effort, I believe we should go, quietly.

This is not about wrong or right, fair or unfair. Life is simply too short to spend our time/effort working in a half-hearted way. We will regret it, others can see/feel it, and the organization deserves someone who can and will produce what it needs.

Clarity

Gaining a clearer view of things is harder than it appears. If greater clarity is a goal, consider this recipe:

1) Be authentically willing to "see more clearly."
2) Be prepared to suspend one's own biases, prejudices, and pre-conceived notions.
3) Seek the perspective of others, even if (especially if) they think, look, and behave differently than oneself.
4) Invest thoughtful reflection upon the varied perspectives one can garner.

5) Triangulate said perspectives against whatever obtainable data exists.
6) Percolate slowly over an extended period of time (we can't microwave "clarity").

Clarity is elusive. Clarity evolves slowly (the stickier the problem, the slower the evolution). Gaining clarity doesn't always "settle the issue." Clarity does, however, inform our thinking and decisions about living and leading well.

Warfighting

Warfighting (1989) is the U.S. Marine Corps book of strategy. I was given a copy of the book by a retired U.S. Marine Corps Colonel. Not only was it an interesting read, I found it to be full of useful guidance for those in leadership positions in any kind setting (not just those in the military).

There were several transferable takeaways for me:

- "Moral forces are difficult to grasp and impossible to quantify…Yet moral forces exert greater influence on the nature and outcome of war than do physical." (p. 16)
- "Intellect without will is worthless, will without intellect is dangerous." -Hans von Seekt
- "We should deal with errors [of junior leaders] leniently; there must be no 'zero defects' mentality. Not only must we not *stifle* boldness or initiative, we must continue to encourage both traits in *spite* of mistakes." (p. 58-59)
- "Because we recognize that no two situations … are the same, our critiques should focus not so much on the actions we took as on why we took those actions and why they brought us the results they did." (p. 63)
- "All commanders should consider the professional development of their subordinates a principal responsibility of command." (p. 66)
- "First and foremost, *in order to generate the tempo of operations we desire and to best cope with the uncertainty, disorder, and fluidity …, command must be decentralized.*" (p. 79)

All are valuable nuggets for leadership thinking and behavior. Moreover, all have resonating connection to the leader's astuteness of the contextual landscape. Truly exceptional leaders seem to be able to see/hear/feel the "whole" better than anyone else in the organization. Daniel Pink (2012) calls this "attunement." Indeed, and it is absolutely critical to our effectiveness as leaders.

Epilogue   The Reason Behind It All

"It's only human,' you cry in defense of any depravity, reaching the stage of self-abasement where you seek to make the concept 'human' mean the weakling, the fool, the rotter, the liar, the failure, the coward, the fraud, and to exile from the human race the hero, the thinker, the producer, the inventor, the strong, the purposeful, the pure—as if 'to feel' were human, but to think were not, as if to fail were human, but to succeed were not, as if corruption were human, but virtue were not—as if the premise of death were proper to man, but the premise of life were not."

- AYN RAND

This discussion of leadership between you and me is now coming to an end. I asked you at the end of the INTRODUCTION to jot down three questions that were at the forefront of your mind as you began reading this book. Please take a look at those three questions and see if any or all were addressed during our time of shared thinking.

All of us want success in life. All of us want to feel effective. But success is defined in a million ways. What is important, at the end of the day, is that we have lived a meaningful life. Brooks (2014) discusses this as being the difference in the resume virtues versus the eulogy virtues.

Kaku (2006), in his book titled *Parallel Worlds*, provides an interesting overview of what we currently know about physics in the 21ˢᵗ century. In it he discusses the Big Bang, quantum physics, astrophysics, nanophysics, string theory, the 11ᵗʰ dimension, and more. Kaku waxes a bit melancholy at the end of the book. He poses the question as to the meaning of it all. He invites us to reflect on the things that actually give life meaning.

Kaku concludes there are four things that provide fundamental meaning to our lives:

1) Work – that is meaningful and substantive, that provides a framework for our lives;
2) Love – that gives us vital and fulfilling connections with others;
3) Using our talent – in ways that honor the gifts with which we have been blessed; and,
4) Legacy – intentionally leaving the world a better place for our having been one its occupants.

Zombies

Dr. Zubin Damania (2013) talks about the disenchantment he felt as a physician. With aspirations of helping others, connecting deeply with others, and feeling self-actualized through medical practice, Dr. Damania entered the profession. Then he learned of the pace, the lack of interpersonal connections with patients, the constant frustration of being overwhelmed, and the demand for "volume" (thus, revenue). He learned that the elements of homogenization and commoditization of service were/are the underlying drivers in healthcare provision.

Interestingly, I have heard my own physician, Dr. Ben Edwards (http://www.veritasmedical.com/ben-edwards), speak of similar frustrations while he conducted his practice in the conventional ways. While both physicians have chosen less commercialized paths by which to serve the healthcare needs of their patients, they allude to a dynamic that is *not* specific to healthcare.

Joel Salatin (2016) is widely known (and published) for his unconventional approach to farming and ranching. The similarity he shares with Drs. Damania and Edwards is that he has chosen and advocates a move away from homogenization and commoditization.

These three professionals have chosen to resist being **zombies** in their chosen vocations. I use the word "zombies" in the sense that is portrayed by Aldous Huxley in *Brave New World* (1932), Suzanne Collins in *The Hunger Games* (2008), and the movie *WALL-E* (2008). In their respective ways each of these works portrays a human existence that is subservient to higher powers (whether in the form of governmental hubris or excessive greed) that seek to de-individualize human beings and to dishonor diversity (in all its forms). The effects are deleterious.

Like Dr. Damania, Dr. Edwards, and Mr. Salatin, I have made the conscious decision to no longer be a zombie, and with respect to my profession as an educator, to no longer being hell-bent on producing zombies.

Respect for individuality, the honoring of differences, the power of relationships, the sustainability of holistic education, the sacredness of interdependence and independence represent the kind of life and work I choose for myself, and would choose for my children, for my grandchildren, and for all the other learners I will yet serve.

What vs Who

Some of my earliest memories are those of answering this question from adults: "What do you want to be when you grow up?"

I went through the usual transitions most young boys do. I can remember being allured by the glamorous professions of policeman (my dad *was* one of those), fireman, etc. I even wanted at one point to be a garbage man. Yep, just think of it, getting to ride, standing up, on the back of those big trucks all day long. Blissful work, indeed! As I grew older, the list changed a bit. I wanted to be a professional athlete, a famous musician, a preacher. But, the skill, the talent, the discipline, the calling seemed somehow absent.

Then, the practical concerns began to set in. What could I do to put food on the table and make the college tuition payment? What could I be that would provide satisfaction as well as reasonable income for my family, for the long haul?

Eventually, the question of *meaning* crept into the calculus of "what I wanted to be when I grew up." Whatever it was needed to be something that had meaning to it, some opportunity to make a difference in the world. I learned over time that the "what" had very little to do with meaning making.

So, the search continued. To this day, I'm not sure I can tell you definitively what I want to be when I grow up. In retrospect, however, those adults early on were asking me the wrong question. I took the bait and continued the trend of asking myself the wrong question through nearly six decades of living. I (and they) shouldn't have been asking, "What do you want to be?"

The right question all along is and should have been, "**WHO** do you want to be?"

That question can be answered from any circumstance or station in life, ir-respective of one's vocational or avocational pursuits. The *meaning* is found in the Who, not the What. We may not get to write every word or sentence or paragraph or chapter in our lives, but we absolutely get to do the editing. And the editing makes all the difference in *who* we are now, and who we become along the way.

Sobering

From time to time, I encounter a concept that takes me aback. Usually, it's not something that is completely foreign to me, but rather it is the skillful framing of a powerful idea. Sometimes those personal "epiphanies" occur in the form of metaphor, sometimes they are captured in some kind of graphic representation, sometimes in the artful stringing together of words.

I recently was brought face-to-face with one of those powerful conceptualizations: **What we teach our children, we teach their children.**

If ever there was a reason to be purposeful, deliberate, and persistent in the choices we make about what we do, why we do it, and how we teach it, that is it. A sobering thought, indeed.

Snapshot

We tend to experience life in the now, in this moment, as if it is a snapshot. Dismay, elation, happiness, grief, pride, love and so many other emotional states seem to envelope us right now, today.

Yet, life plays out rather like a movie. To be sure, the moments, events, the experiences have a specific date and time attached to them (just like a snapshot). However, when we think of and view our lives as a movie, we have tremendous power to affect the "story" as it unfolds.

We write the script. We greatly influence the way the story unfolds. We have ultimate control of how the main character – you/me - is developed, we have the power to foster healthy relationships (or not), we can impact our world through acts of service (or not), we can gently engage with the planet upon which we live (or not), and we can choose to commune authentically with the God of our understanding (or not).

The snapshots count, but the movie matters most.

Lights, camera, ...

Transcendent

We can transcend our biases, our weaknesses, our learned prejudices, our pre-conceived notions, and our blind spots of ignorance.

But we can do so only if we're willing. Willing to learn, that is.

Boldacious Leaders

We've all followed leaders, lots of them. Some, however, stand out as exceptional in our minds. I like to think of those extra special kinds of

leaders as *boldacious* (yep, another made up word). Here are some of the things about boldacious leaders that make them so extraordinary:

- They help us see better futures for ourselves, both individually and collectively.
- They *invite* us to come along on their journey (they don't demand compliant followership).
- They are passionate about the journey they're on, and it's contagious.
- They accept us just as we are, then invest in us like crazy to move us toward our best possibilities.
- They communicate consistently and persistently about where they think we ought to be going and why they think it's important to go there.
- They genuinely care about us, and it shows.

Sign me up, Captain. I'll gladly play on Team Boldacious.

Anomalies

"Anomaly" is an interesting word that means that something or someone is different from what is normal or expected. Some words that have similar meaning are irregular, rare, and abnormal.

It's unfortunate that leaders
who speak plainly,

who model integrity,
who exemplify honesty,
who are service-oriented,
who consistently adhere to principle,
who willingly own their decisions (and mistakes),
are often viewed as *anomalies*.

Wouldn't it be nice if those leadership anomalies............weren't?

Significance

Our significance in life is directly proportional to the service we provide to others.

When we are focused on serving others we make their lives better, often without their even knowing it. These acts of service can be small or great, they can be ongoing or ad hoc. Those served by us can be loved and well-known, or they can be complete strangers. Service has no limits or boundaries.

No credentials or specialized training is required to serve. We can all provide service to others regardless of our age, our level of education, or our station in life.

When serving ourselves we become less; when serving others we become more ... significant.

Deference

Deference is manifested in a number of ways:

Respectfulness   *Humility*   *Intense listening*

Empathy   *Expressed vulnerability*   *Serving*

Transparent interactions   *Sharing*   *Giving*

Many of my personal heroes commit most, if not all, of these acts of deference as a matter of course. In fact, as I reflect on their behaviors it is apparent to me that they have simply turned these notable acts/behaviors into habits. Pretty nice list of things to work on for getting better, every day, on purpose, huh?

Best Most

An intriguing question came to my attention recently: Do the people that know me the best respect me the most?

That's an interesting question when we reflect on the number of high profile and public figures in history who had sparkling public reputations but were held in disdain by the people closest to them. We can easily think of leaders of high regard who privately engaged in hateful treatment of others, who spoke disparagingly of opponents, who connived to undercut or ruin those who disagreed with them. It is not hard to conjure up memories of ministers whose private lives were not at all aligned to the values they preached from the pulpit. I imagine that every one of us can think of a boss in our past (or present) whose public persona was sparkling, but whose words/deeds behind closed doors revealed a far less attractive character.

The issue at hand can be captured in one powerful word, I think - integrity. That word speaks directly to the level of alignment between our true beliefs/values and the way we manifest those beliefs/values *every* moment of our lives (not just when "on the stage").

So, the question begs: **Do the people that know me the best respect me the most?**

Forever Work

Work comes in all shapes and sizes: physical labor, mental processing, paper shuffling, monitoring, selling, supervising, harvesting, etc. The list is endless, and the impact is mostly temporal.

Some work, however, is *forever* work. This is the work we do that has impact, that lasts beyond our lifetime, even beyond our generation. Forever work is not about putting food on the table, making the mortgage payment, or funding the vacation. Forever work is about legacy, and it's always grounded in our relationships.

Of course we have to work for the almighty dollar (most of us, anyway) in order to make ends meet, but we must also work for that bigger picture - the forever work.

Essentially, it's the work of passing along values, ways of thinking, and ways of being. And how do we transmit those critical elements? Through strong and carefully attended relationships with those we love (and, derivatively, with the ones *they* love).

It is important to assess how we dole out our time, our effort, our thinking, and our attention with respect to those two kinds of work - the temporal kind and the forever kind.

And, we should probably ask ourselves if we're happy with the apportionment. If not, today is the day to make adjustments. Forever depends on it.

Summative or Formative?

Assessment is a tool/process by which we assign value to someone's/something's performance or knowledge or skills or prowess or wealth, based on some chosen measurement (the metric often chosen by someone else). I know! There sure are a lot of "somes" in that sentence. Adds to the clarity, huh?

Summative assessments are snapshots taken of that someone/something on a rather infrequent time frame, often annually. For students, we have become accustomed to testing them once per year with a really long test, presumably to find out whether they have learned what they were supposed to over that year of time. For us big people, it might be a measurement of our net worth on March 1 of each year or our body weight on each January 1 (ouch!). A summative assessment is a little like an autopsy, an after-the-fact, backward-looking evaluation.

Formative assessments are ongoing evaluations, taken hourly, daily, weekly, or monthly. Formative assessments are more like a movie-in-progress (as opposed to a snapshot). Formative assessments can be likened to frequent, regular monitoring of personal health markers (like weight, blood pressure, cholesterol levels, pulse rates, etc.). They measure current progress, with an eye on what growth/development/learning needs to happen next - the next minute, the next hour, the next day, the next month. Generally, formative assessment is viewed in the context of cumulative progress to date.

Summative assessment is most often used to compare or sort or rank someone/something with some other someones/somethings. Formative assessments are most useful when we're trying to get some sense of authentic and current growth/performance, as individuals or organizations - it's our progress being measured against our own previous progress or performance.

How, then, shall we choose to measure our lives? Formative for me, please.

Life Editing

Miller (2009) makes the case that we edit our own lives, we write our own stories. To be sure, things happen in life that are well beyond our control. Generally, however, we have the power to be who we want to be, to proceed as we want to proceed, and to react to prosperity/adversity as we wish. We do, in fact, "edit" our lives.

We continue writing the story of our lives each day.

The authors of the best stories (both the literary kind and the life-story kind) do their writing with an eye on both past and future. They connect with the pages and chapters past fluidly as they craft the pages and chapters

future. Knowing they can't unwrite the pages already published, they are fully aware that they can take the next pages and chapters in any direction they wish.

Write well the next pages and chapters, as you wish them to be.

Fulfillment

In ending this book, let me extend an invitation to you: Examine your work and life against Kaku's (2006) four assertions about the meaning of life (i.e., Work, Love, Talent Usage, and Legacy) and decide if you're happy with the choices you've made so far.

If Kaku is correct and life is provided meaning through the exercise of those four constructs, then those of us in leadership roles are afforded great opportunities for living meaningful lives.

Fulfillment is really an art, when you think about it. It's not something we can purchase or inherit. Our fulfillment is something we build personally, over a lifetime. And, we never get finished. On the day we die, we will still be able to view that as work yet unfinished.

Yet, the process of thinking deeply about focusing our lives, our time, our effort, and our tangible resources on the things that have real *meaning* is the essence of crafting a fulfilling life. And it has everything to do with effectively exercising our leadership skills, in a praxical way.

References

Alexander, C. (1979). *The timeless way of building*. New York: Oxford University Press.

Badaracco, J. (2002). *Leading quietly: An unorthodox guide to doing the right thing*. Boston: Harvard Business School Press.

Bass, B.M., & Avolio, B.J. (1994) *Improving Organizational Effectiveness Through Transformational Leadership*. Thousand Oaks, CA: Sage Publications.

Bass, B.M. (1990). *Bass and Stodgill's handbook of leadership*. New York: Free Press.

Blanchard, K., & Hodges, P. (2005). *Lead like Jesus:Lessons from the greatest leadership role model of all times*. Nashville, TN: W Publishing Group.

Block, P. (1993). *Stewardship: Choosing service over self-interest*. San Francisco, CA: Berrett-Kohler.

Block, P. (2002). *The answer to how is yes: Acting on what matters*. San Francisco, CA: Berrett-Koehler Publishers, Inc.

Block, P. (2008). *Community: The structure of belonging*. San Francisco, CA: Berrett-Koehler Publishers, Inc.

Bloom, B. S., Englehart, M. D., Furst, E. J., Hill, W. H., Krathwohl, D. R. (1956). *Taxonomy of educational objectives: The classification of educational goals. Handbook I: Cognitive domain.* New York: David McKay Company.

Bolman, L. G., & Deal, T. E. (1991). *Reframing organizations: Artistry, choice, and leadership.* San Francisco, CA: Jossey-Bass.

Bolman, L.G., & Deal, T. E. (2006). *The wizard and the warrior: Leading with passion and power.* San Francisco, CA: Jossey-Bass.

Bono, J. E., & Ilies, R. (2006). Charisma, positive emotions and mood contagion. *The Leadership Quarterly, 17 (2006),* 317-334.

Bossidy, L., & Charan, R. (2002). *Execution: The discipline of getting things done.* New York: Crown Business.

Brady, M (2003). *The wisdom of listening.* Somerville, MA: Wisdom publications.

Brooks, D. (2014). *David Brooks: Should you live for your resume...or your eulogy?* (Video file.) Retrieved from https://www.ted.com/talks/david_brooks_should_you_live_for_your_resume_or_your_eulogy?language=en

Bruner, J. (1987). *Actual minds, possible worlds.* Boston, MA: Fellows of Harvard College.

Buckingham, M., & Clifton, D. O. (2001). *Now, discover your strengths.* New York: The Free Press.

Buckingham, M., & Coffman, C. (1999). *First, break all the rules: What the world's greatest managers do differently.* New York: Simon & Schuster.

Chopra, D. (2009). *Reinventing the body, resurrecting the soul: How to create a new you.* New York: Harmony Books.

Christensen, C. M., Allworth, J., & Dillon, K. (2012). *How will you measure your life?* New York: Harper Business.

Christensen, D. (2014). *Transforming Schools…Changing Minds + Changing Practices + Changing Leading.* Keynote at TASA Mission: School Transformation, March 25, 2014, Marriott Hotel, Round Rock, Texas.

Cloud, H. (2010). *Necessary endings: The employees, businesses, and relationships that all of us have to give up in order to move forward.* New York: HarperBusiness.

Collins, S. (2008). *The Hunger Games (Book 1).* New York: Scholastic, Inc.

Costa, A.L., & Kallick, B. (2000). *Discovering and exploring habits of mind.* Alexandria, VA: ASCD.

Covey, S. M. R. (2006). *The speed of trust: The one thing that changes everything.* New York: Free Press.

Covey, S. R. (2004). *The 8th habit: From effectiveness to greatness.* New York: Free Press.

Csikszentmihalyi, M. (1997). *Finding flow: The psychology of engagement with everyday life.* New York: BasicBooks.

Damania, Z. (2013). *Zubin Damania: Are zombie doctors taking over America?* (Video file.) Retrieved from https://www.youtube.com/watch?v=QLqrjLBV95o

Duhigg, C. (2012). *The power of habit: Why we do what we do in life and business.* New York: Random House.

Earley, P. C., & Mosakowski, E. (2004). Cultural intelligence. *Harvard Business Review, 82* (10), 139-146.

Edwards, B. (2015). From personal correspondence on October 29, 2015.

Erickson, H. L. (2002). *Concept-based curriculum and instruction: Teaching beyond the facts.* Thousand Oaks, CA: Corwin Press, Inc.

Farber, S. (2016). *"Choose to be extreme."* Retrieved from http://www.stevefarber.com/extreme-leadership/

Fisher, R., Ury, W., & Patton, B. (1991). *Getting to yes: Negotiating agreement without giving in. 2nd Edition.* New York: The Penguin Group.

Frankl, V.E. (1992). *Man's search for meaning: An introduction to logotherapy.* Boston, MA: Beacon Press.

Friedman, T. (2005). *The world is flat: A brief history of the twenty-first century.* New York: Farrar, Straus and Giroux.

Gardner, H. (1993). *Multiple intelligences: The theory in practice.* New York: BasicBooks.

Gardner, J. W. (1990). *On leadership.* New York: The Free Press.

Goleman, D. (1994). *Emotional intelligence: Why it matters more than IQ.* New York: Bantam.

Goleman, D. (1998). What makes a leader? *Harvard Business Review 76 (6),* 93-102.

Goleman, D. (2008). *Social intelligence: The revolutionary new science of human relationships.* New York: Bantam Books.

Henry, T. (2013). *Die empty: Unleash your best work everyday.* New York: Portfolio/Penguin.

Horn, J. (2015). *TASA Mentor Training*, January 24, 2015, Austin Convention Center, Austin, Texas.

Houston, P. D., & Sokolow, S. L. (2006). *The spiritual dimension of leadership: 8 key principles to leading more effectively*. Thousand Oaks, CA: Corwin Press.

Huxley, A. (1932). *Brave new world*. Garden City, NY: Doubleday, Doran.

Hyman, M. (2015). *Inflammation: How to cool the fire inside you that's making you fat and diseased*. (Video file.)Retrieved from http://drhyman.com/blog/2012/01/27/inflammation-how-to-cool-the-fire-inside-you-thats-making-you-fat-and-diseased/

Kaku, M. (2006). *Parallel worlds: A journey through creation, higher dimensions, and the future of the cosmos*. New York: Doubleday. Publishing.

Lustig, R. H. (2009). *Sugar: The bitter truth*. (Video file.) Retrieved at https://www.youtube.com/watch?v=dBnniua6-oM

Mercola, J. (2015). *Obesity rates continue to climb*. Article retrieved November 11, 2015 from http://articles.mercola.com/sites/articles/archive/2015/11/25/obesity-rates-continue-to-climb.aspx?e_cid=20151125Z1_DNL_art_1&utm_source=dnl&utm_medium=email&utm_content=art1&utm_campaign=20151125Z1&et_cid=DM91015&et_rid=1232334292).

Miller, D. (2009). *A million miles in a thousand years: What I learned while editing my life*. Nashville, TN: Thomas Nelson, Inc.

Mitchell, R. (2014, March 4). *Consequence is no coincidence*. [Facebook status update]. Retrieved from https://www.facebook.com/DrFitt/posts/713417065391808

Morgan, G. (1998). *Images of organization.* San Francisco, CA: Berrett-Koehler Publishers, Inc.

Moxley, R. S. (2000). *Leadership and spirit: Breathing new vitality and energy into individuals and organizations.* San Francisco, CA: Jossey-Bass, Inc.

Pink, D. H. (2012). *To sell is human: The surprising truth about moving others.* New York: Riverhead Books.

Powell, C. L. (1995). *My American journey.* New York: Ballantine.

Rock, D. (2008). *SCARF : A brain-based model for collaborating with and influencing others.* NeuroLeadershipJournal.

Salatin, J. (2016). *Joel Salatin : Can real food from real farms lead to real health ?* (Video file.) Retrieved from http://www.tedmed.com/talks/show?id=7342

Sample, S. B. (2002). *The contrarian's guide to leadership.* San Francisco, CA: Jossey-Bass.

Scharmer, C. O. (2009). *Theory U: Leading from the future as it emerges.* Cambridge, MA: Society for Organizational Learning.

Seligman, M. (2002). *Authentic Happiness: Using the new positive psychology to realize your potential for lasting fulfillment.* New York: Free Press.

Senge, P.M. (1990). *The fifth discipline: The art and practice of the learning organization.* New York: Doubleday.

Senge, P., Scharmer, C. O., Jaworski, J., & Flowers, B. S. (2005). *Presence: An exploration of profound change in people, organizations, and society.* New York: Currency Books.

Sinek, S. (2010). *Simon Sinek: How great leaders inspire action.* (Video file.) Retrieved from https://www.youtube.com/watch?v=qp0HIF3Sfl4

Sowell, T. (2013). *Intellectuals and race.* New York: Basic Books.

Stanto, A., Morris, J., Lasseter, J., Docter, P., Reardon, J., Newman, T., Eggleston, R., ... Walt Disney Home Entertainment (Firm). (2008). *WALL-E.* Burbank, Calif: Walt Disney Home Entertainment.

Sutton, R. I. (2010). *Good boss, bad boss: How to be the best...and learn from the worst.* New York: Business Plus.

Taylor, W. C., & Labarre, P. (2008). *Mavericks at work: Why the most original minds in business win.* New York: HarperCollins.

U.S. Marine Corps. (1989). *Warfighting: The U.S. Marine Corps book of strategy.* New York: Currency Paperback by Doubleday.

Wheatley, M. J. (2006). *Leadership and the new science: Discovering order in a chaotic world, 3rd Edition.* San Francisco, CA: Berrett-Koehler Publishers, Inc.

Whitaker, T. (2012). *What great principals do differently: Eighteen things that matter most (2nd Ed.).* New York: Routledge.

Wilber, K. (1996). *A brief history of everything.* Boston, MA: Shambhala Publications, Inc.

Made in the USA
Middletown, DE
09 August 2017